Realistic Construction Models You Can Make

By Luc St-Amour

Fox
Chapel Publishing Co. Inc.
1970 Broad Street • East Petersburg, PA 17520 • www.carvingworld.com

Publisher: Alan Giagnocavo
Editor: Ayleen Stellhorn
Desktop Specialist: Linda L. Eberly, Eberly Designs Inc.
Cover Photography: Robert Polett

ISBN # 1–56523–152–X
Library of Congress Card Number: 00–111564

To order your copy of this book,
please send check or money order
for the cover price plus $3.00 shipping to:
Fox Books
1970 Broad Street
East Petersburg, PA 17520

Or visit us on the web at
www.carvingworld.com

Manufactured in the USA

IMPORTANT NOTICE TO PARENTS AND READERS

The models in this book are designed as display models only. Models contain small parts that may break and be swallowed by a young child, posing a choking hazard. If you wish to make this collection for children ages five and older, please inquire about the book *Making Construction Vehicles For Kids,* available from this publisher.

For my wonderful wife and children

who are always there to give me

love, support and inspiration.

Acknowledgments

I wish to thank all the people who have contributed to this project, especially my family and friends.

I would also like to thank the "Autodesk" company, who supplied me with the "Autocad" computer software.

I dedicate this book to all the people who are young at heart - people who still believe that dreams can come true and that everyday life is full of little joys.

I hope that these models give you as much pleasure (making them or giving them) as I had creating them for you.

Luc St-Amour

Table of Contents

Introduction 1

How to use this book 2

Tools and Techniques... 3

Helpful Hints... 4

Loader 12

Dozer... 29

Dozer Loader... 44

Excavator... 60

Grader.. 77

Skidder... 92

Grapple Skidder 105

Backhoe 121

Introduction

This book is for all those who enjoy building wooden models. In this edition you will learn to build fascinating construction vehicles. Our main objective in creating this book was to help you attain the best possible results in reproducing these vehicles as easily and simply as possible. Building them will require patience, know-how and, most importantly, the proper tools.

So, for those who enjoy detail and precision, you'll love building these models using the easy and accurate methods suggested in this book.

You will note that special care has been taken to provide you with as many explanations and instructions as possible. All patterns are full size and easily transfered onto wood. Easy-to-follow assembly drawings are also included for each model.

Please keep in mind the most important aspect of woodworking - safety! And don't forget to read all instructions before you begin.

I wish you the best of luck with your projects.

Please note: The models you can build with this book are not toys. (There are many small parts that can easily break and may be swallowed by young children.) They have been specifically designed as display models only. If you wish to make this line of construction vehicles for a child, you can buy the book entitled *Making Construction Vehicles For Kids* by the same author.

How to use this book

1. Start by reading through the book to get familiar with its contents.

2. Make the two jigs shown on page 4 and 5.

3. Use the materials list to cut all the parts required for a particuliar model. Label the parts with a pencil using their corresponding number (e.g. L1, L2)

4. You have been supplied with two sets of patterns for each model. The first set is found with the instructions and includes all parts. The second set can be found in the appendix and includes only those parts complicated enough to require a pattern. Using scissors, cut out the second set of patterns needed to make the model you have chosen to build.

5. Attach the pattern to the proper piece of stock.

6. Cut and sand the finished parts.

7. Mark drill holes, if required, and remove the pattern.

8. When all the parts are completed, follow the step-by-step assembly drawings to complete your model.

Tools and Techniques

Because of the complexity of the models, the use of power tools is a must. They will not only give you the precision needed but will also save you an enormous amount of time.

To make some parts you will be required to make intricate inside cuts. The best tool for this task is the scroll saw. A drill press must also be used to drill holes in the centre of the dowel. (A hand drill is not suitable for this task.)

For sanding purposes, you will need power sanders to save you time and give better results.

The wood needed to make these projects varies in thicknesses which are not standard. This means you will need to use a thickness planner and a bandsaw to re-saw and bring the wood to the specified thickness. (Some of you may have access to these tools at school, from friends or at a store.)

Accessories Needed

- Drill bit set (1/16" to 1/2")
- Brad point bits (1/8" and 1/4")
- Flat drill bit set (3/8" to 1")
- Measuring tape
- Combination square
- Sanding drum set
- Wood vice
- Assorted c-clamps
- Scriber
- Wood glue
- Wood file
- Pencil and eraser
- 12" ruler (clear recommended)
- 1/2" wide masking tape
- Compass
- Circle template

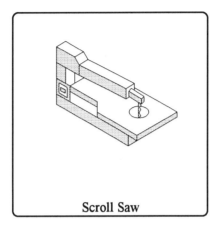

Scroll Saw

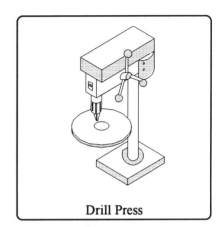

Drill Press

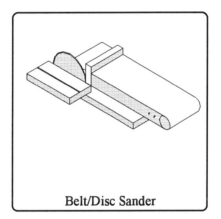

Belt/Disc Sander

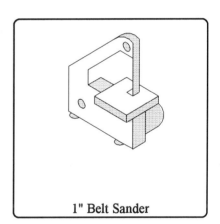

1" Belt Sander

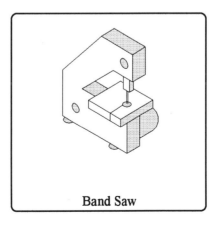

Band Saw

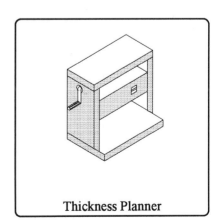

Thickness Planner

Helpful Hints

HINT #1 MAKING A CHANFER ON THE WHEELS

Make a jig to round the edges of your wheels by cutting a bolt (removing the hexagon) and assembling it, as shown. Use this jig with your drill press.

Please note: Drill a 1/4" diameter hole in your wheels to install on this jig. When you finish sanding the wheels, re-drill the 1/4" diameter holes, this time using a 17/64" drill bit as specified in your plans.

Materials needed to make this jig

(1) 1/4" diameter bolt, 1 3/4" long

(2) 1/4" int. diameter flat washers

(1) 1/4" diameter nut

Illustration 1

View of parts necessary to make the sanding jig.

Illustration 2

Insert unthreaded end of bolt into drill press. Tighten chuck and slide on washer, wheel and 2nd washer. Secure everything using the nut.

Illustration 3

You are now ready to make the chanfer on the wheel. Start your drill press at low to medium r.p.m.s. Then, use a wood file to round the edges of your wheel. Use sandpaper to get a smooth finish.

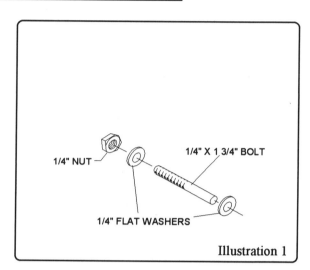

1/4" NUT

1/4" X 1 3/4" BOLT

1/4" FLAT WASHERS

Illustration 1

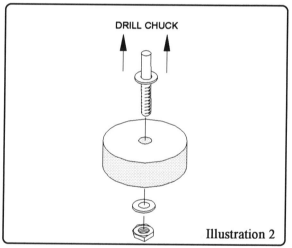

DRILL CHUCK

Illustration 2

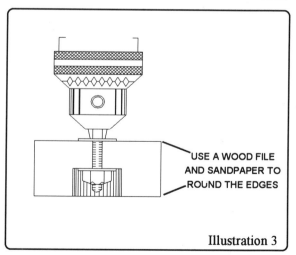

USE A WOOD FILE AND SANDPAPER TO ROUND THE EDGES

Illustration 3

HINT #2 MAKE YOUR OWN SPECIAL DRILLING JIGS

To make the models shown in this book you must be able to drill a hole perfectly in the centre of a dowel. You can do this using your drill press and the special homemade jig shown here.

You will need to make 3 jigs to hold the cylinders (dowels) in position. Making these jigs will save you a lot of time!

Instructions for drilling dowels can be found below.

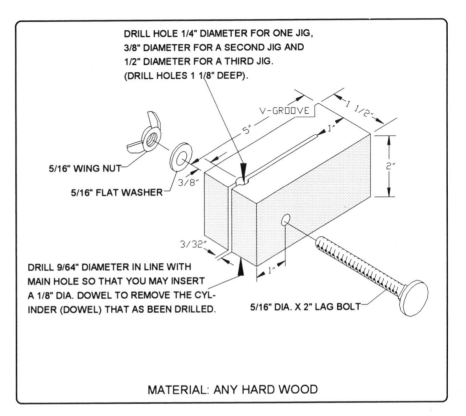

DRILL HOLE 1/4" DIAMETER FOR ONE JIG, 3/8" DIAMETER FOR A SECOND JIG AND 1/2" DIAMETER FOR A THIRD JIG. (DRILL HOLES 1 1/8" DEEP).

V-GROOVE

5/16" WING NUT

5/16" FLAT WASHER

DRILL 9/64" DIAMETER IN LINE WITH MAIN HOLE SO THAT YOU MAY INSERT A 1/8" DIA. DOWEL TO REMOVE THE CYLINDER (DOWEL) THAT AS BEEN DRILLED.

5/16" DIA. X 2" LAG BOLT

MATERIAL: ANY HARD WOOD

HINT #3 HOW TO DRILL A HOLE PERFECTLY IN THE CENTRE OF A DOWEL

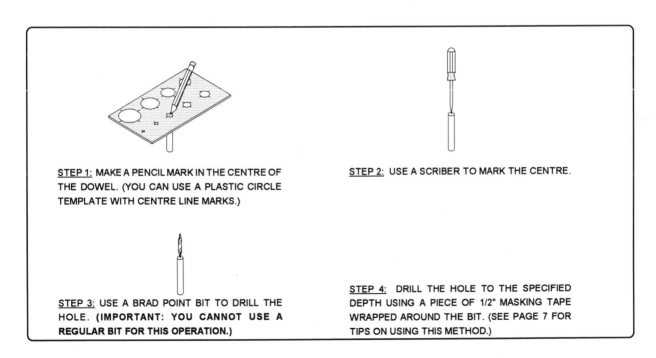

STEP 1: MAKE A PENCIL MARK IN THE CENTRE OF THE DOWEL. (YOU CAN USE A PLASTIC CIRCLE TEMPLATE WITH CENTRE LINE MARKS.)

STEP 2: USE A SCRIBER TO MARK THE CENTRE.

STEP 3: USE A BRAD POINT BIT TO DRILL THE HOLE. (IMPORTANT: YOU CANNOT USE A REGULAR BIT FOR THIS OPERATION.)

STEP 4: DRILL THE HOLE TO THE SPECIFIED DEPTH USING A PIECE OF 1/2" MASKING TAPE WRAPPED AROUND THE BIT. (SEE PAGE 7 FOR TIPS ON USING THIS METHOD.)

HINT # 4 HOW TO MAKE A TRACK ASSEMBLY

Step 1

Trace four lines across
surface, as shown.
(Note: See patterns for guide lines.)

Step 2

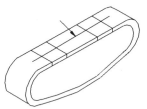

Trace a line down the centre,
as shown.

Step 3

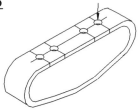

Drill four 3/8" holes on centre
marks through first surface only.

Step 4

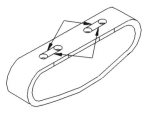

Using a sharp knife, cut lines
tangent to holes, as shown.

Step 5

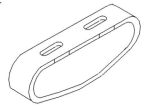

Opening properly cut.

Step 6

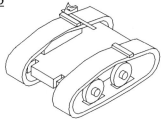

Assemble track assembly, then
glue two track threads perpendicular
to sides using a square to guide you.

Step 7

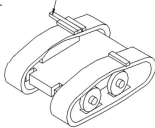

Glue the rest of the track threads using
a spacer that is the same width as track threads.
(Note: Do not glue this spacer.)

Step 8

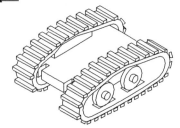

When you are done glueing all the
threads, wait for them to dry before
doing a final sanding.

HINT # 5 MAKING A SHOVEL THE EASY WAY

Step 1

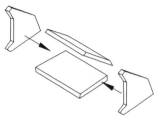

Glue shovel sides to shovel,
top and bottom, as shown.

Step 2

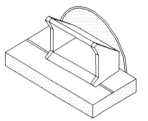

Sand the back surface to
get a straight face.

Step 3

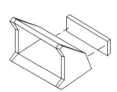

Glue on shovel back. Note: Shovel top,
bottom and back are cut oversized to allow sanding.

Step 4

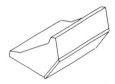

Do a final sanding to get
your finished shovel.

HINT # 6 HOW TO DRILL HOLES TO THE SPECIFIED DEPTH

To get holes to specified depth, use a
piece of masking tape (1/2" wide or less).
Wrap it around drill bit, as shown.

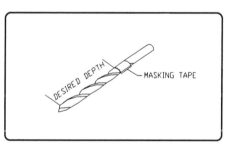

Also, always use a piece of scrap wood (e.g.
plywood) under the part that you are drilling.
You will achieve better results, while preventing
breakage that may occur otherwise.

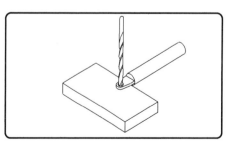

HINT #7 HOW TO MAKE THE DIFFERENT PISTONS AND CYLINDERS REQUIRED

All the pistons, cylinders and pins are made by using maple dowels. It is recommend that you purchase a few of each. The diameters of these dowels are 1/8", 1/4", 3/8" and 1/2". They are usually sold in 3- or 4- foot lengths.

When making these models you will need to make two different types of pistons and cylinders. Each requiring just a few steps. In a short time, you should be able to make them quickly and easily.

The following is the first type of piston and cylinder you will need to make.

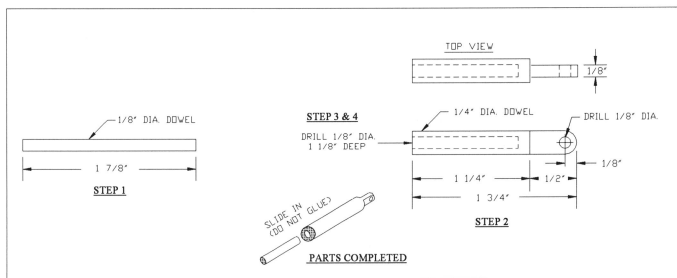

Step 1	Cut piston (1/8" diameter dowel) to length. In this case 1 7/8" long.
Step 2	Cut cylinder (1/4" diameter dowel) to length. In this case 1 3/4" long.
Step 3	Trace and mark the centre of the cylinder (1/4" diameter dowel) using the method shown on page 5.
Step 4	Using the jig shown on page 5, hold the cylinder in position and drill the 1/8" diameter hole to proper depth- in this case 1 1/8" deep.
Step 5	Make a guideline at the opposite end of cylinder. In this case, 1/2" away from the end of dowel.
Step 6	Using your 1" wide disc sander, sand this end flat to 1/8" thickness. See drawing of completed part above.
Step 7	Drill the 1/8" diameter hole.
Step 8	Round off the corners to complete the piston and cylinder assembly.

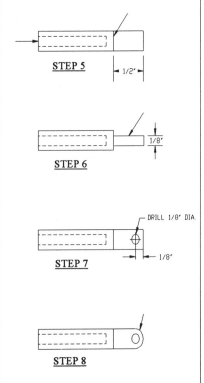

The following is an example of the second type of piston and cylinder you will need to make. The only difference between the two types, is that the first has a 1/8" flat end, and this one has a 1/8" diameter end.

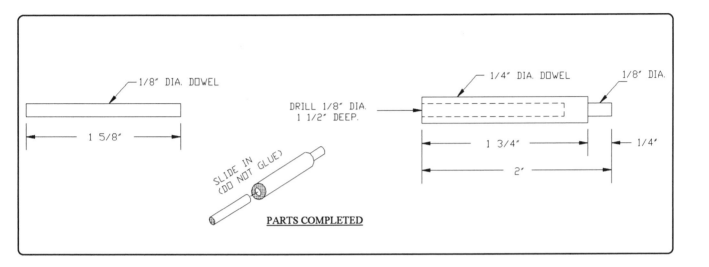

Follow the same steps as on the previous page until step 6. At this stage, sand a 1/8" diameter, using the method shown below.

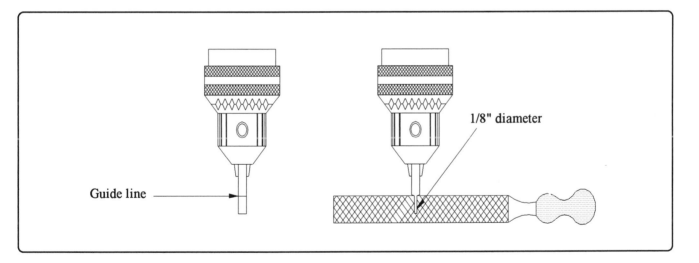

Insert dowel into drill chuck, as shown above. Using a wood file, sand dowel until you get the 1/8" diameter required, using your guideline to help you. It is recommended that you check your diameter often to make sure you don't remove too much material. To test your diameter, use a piece of scrap wood in which you have drilled a 1/8" diameter hole, then check for proper fit.

HINT # 8 TRANSFERING THE GUIDELINES FROM PATTERNS

IMPORTANT: This section applies to these parts only: • The cabin sides
                                                            • The tracks

Transfer guidelines, as shown below.

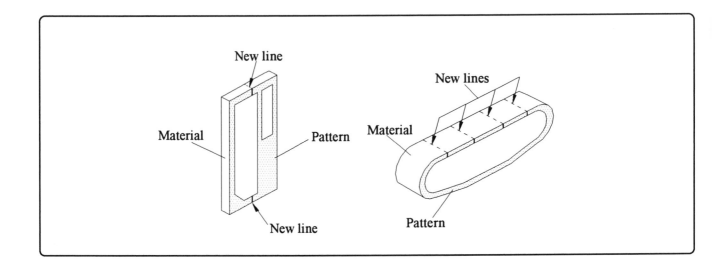

HINT # 9 YOU MUST MODIFY THE DOORS FOR THEM TO OPEN

When doors and cabin sides are cut, there must be a small gap between them. Also, to ensure that they will open and close properly, a section of the door must be sanded to a 45 degree angle. See drawing below to see how this is done.

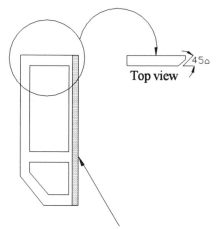

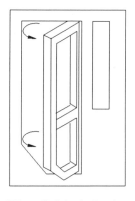

Top view

Lightly sand exterior corner
of door at a 45 degree angle.

When finished, the door
should open, as shown.

LOADER

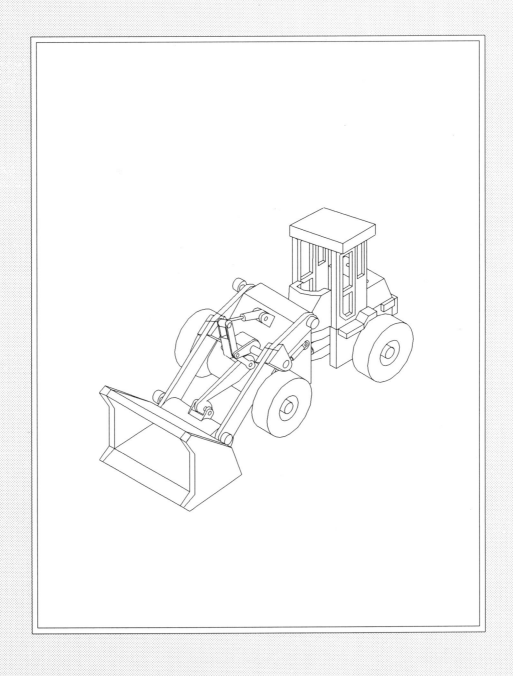

General Instructions - Loader

1- Start by cutting materials needed by following the list of materials, paying attention to the rough and finished size. **Identify the parts as they are cut.**

Please note: Different types of wood can be used for the various parts. It is suggested, however, that hard wood be used, since many of the parts would be much too fragile if using soft wood. We have used a combination of pine, maple and oak to give the models a nice contrast!

2- Remove the full-size patterns found in the appendix. Cut them out, leaving approximately 1/16" all around, and place on the proper piece of wood. Patterns can be secured to wood using either spray adhesive or rubber ciment. If using the latter, cut and sand the part first to finished size. If drilling is required, mark the hole by inserting a scriber or nail through the pattern into the wood. Remove the pattern before drilling.

You should have no trouble determining which surface to attach most of the patterns. Some parts, however, can be confusing since the pattern could fit on more than one surface. The drawings below indicate exactly which surface to attach the patterns for these parts.

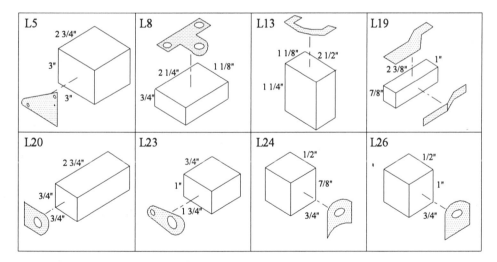

3- Look at the full-size drawing sheets to finish parts L16, L20 and L27.

4- Parts L8, L16, L19, L23, L24, L25 and L26 will need additional cuts and details. Please refer to the Additional Information pages to complete these parts.

5- Using maple dowels, make all pins, shafts, etc.

6- Follow the assembly drawings to complete your model.

List of Materials - Loader

Part	T	W	L	Material	Qty.	*
L1	1/4"	2 1/4"	3 1/4"	oak	1	R
L2	1/4"	2 1/4"	3 1/4"	oak	1	R
L3	1/4"	1 1/4"	2 7/8"	oak	1	R
L4	1/4"	2 1/2"	3 1/4"	oak	1	R
L5	3"	2 3/4"	3"	pine	1	F
L6	1/2"	2 1/2"	6 1/8"	pine	2	R
L7	3/4"	2 1/2"	5"	pine	1	R
L8	3/4"	1 1/8"	2 1/4"	maple	1	R
L9	1/4"	2"	5"	pine	2	R
L10	1/4"	1 7/8"	4 1/2"	pine	1	F
L11	1/8"	1 1/2"	5"	pine	1	F
L12	1/4"	2 3/4"	4 1/2"	pine	1	F
L13	1 1/4"	1 1/8"	2 1/2"	pine	1	R
L14	1/4"	2 3/4"	3"	pine	2	R

Part	T	W	L	Material	Qty.	*
L15	1/4"	2 7/8"	2 1/8"	pine	1	F
L16	1 1/4"	2 3/4"	2 3/4"	pine	1	F
L17	1/4"	1/2"	1"	oak	2	F
L18	1/2"	1 1/2"	3 1/2"	oak	1	R
L19	7/8"	1"	2 3/8"	pine	2	R
L20	3/4"	3/4"	2 3/4"	maple	1	F
L21	1/8"	1 1/4"	1 1/8"	maple	4	R
L22	1/4"	1 5/8"	5 3/4"	maple	2	R
L23	3/4"	1"	1 3/4"	maple	1	R
L24	1/2"	3/4"	7/8"	maple	1	R
L25	1/2"	1"	2 7/8"	maple	1	R
L26	1/2"	3/4"	1"	maple	1	R
L27	1"	2 1/2" DIA.		oak	4	F
L28	1/4"	5/8"	2 1/2"	maple	1	R

T = Thickness
W = Width
L = Length

R = Rough size
F = Finished size

Instructions:

R= Rough sizes, the material is cut oversized so you have ample room to apply the pattern on the surface. Sanding is not required at this point.

F = Finished Size: Cut and sand parts to finished size.

Full-Sized Patterns: Set One

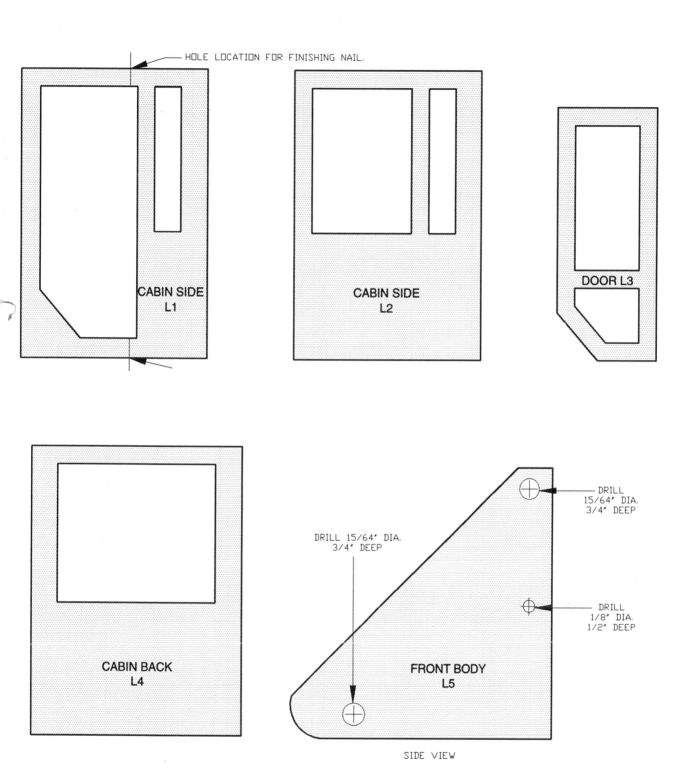

HOLE LOCATION FOR FINISHING NAIL.

CABIN SIDE
L1

CABIN SIDE
L2

DOOR L3

CABIN BACK
L4

DRILL 15/64" DIA.
3/4" DEEP

DRILL
15/64" DIA.
3/4" DEEP

DRILL
1/8" DIA.
1/2" DEEP

FRONT BODY
L5

SIDE VIEW

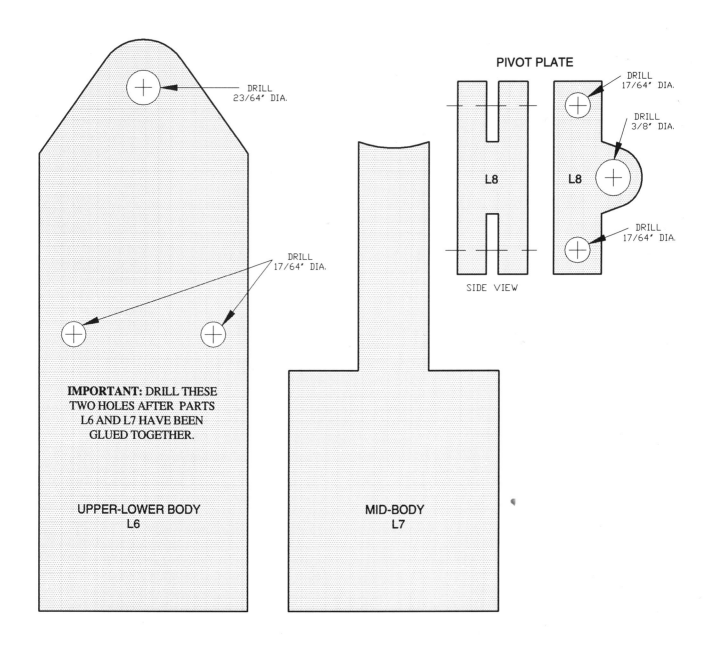

PIVOT PLATE

DRILL
17/64" DIA.

DRILL
3/8" DIA.

L8   L8

DRILL
17/64" DIA.

SIDE VIEW

DRILL
23/64" DIA.

DRILL
17/64" DIA.

IMPORTANT: DRILL THESE
TWO HOLES AFTER PARTS
L6 AND L7 HAVE BEEN
GLUED TOGETHER.

UPPER-LOWER BODY
L6

MID-BODY
L7

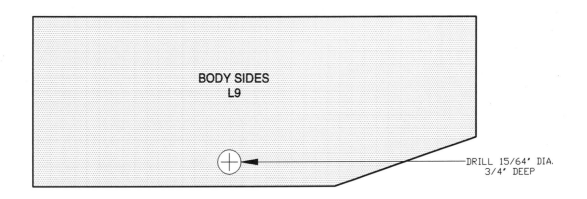

BODY SIDES
L9

DRILL 15/64" DIA.
3/4" DEEP

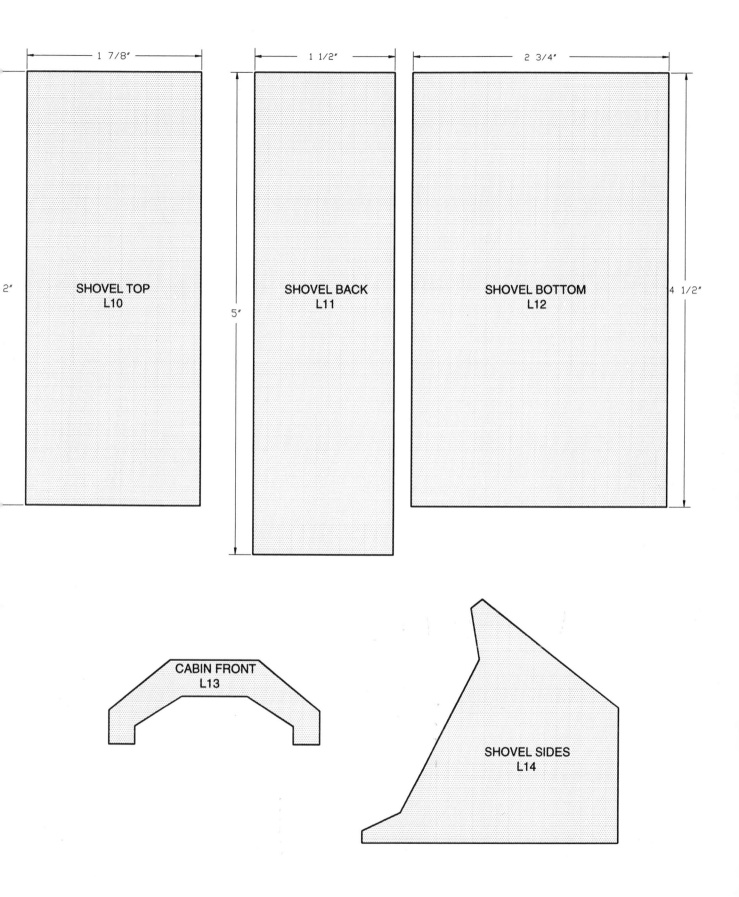

1 7/8″

SHOVEL TOP
L10

2″

1 1/2″

SHOVEL BACK
L11

5″

2 3/4″

SHOVEL BOTTOM
L12

4 1/2″

CABIN FRONT
L13

SHOVEL SIDES
L14

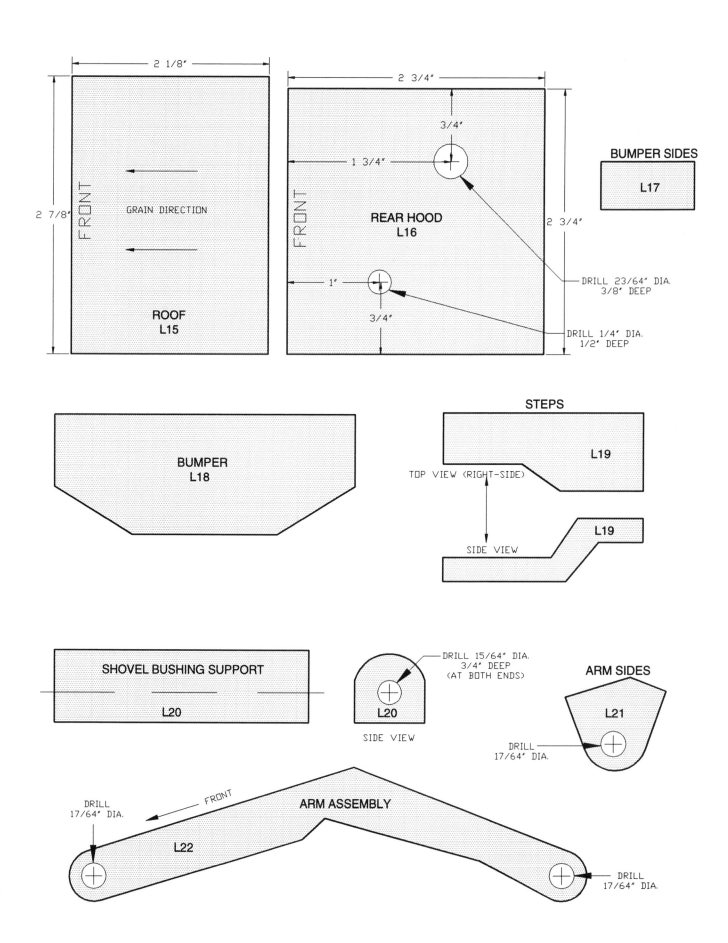

2 1/8"

FRONT

GRAIN DIRECTION

2 7/8"

ROOF
L15

2 3/4"

FRONT

3/4"

1 3/4"

REAR HOOD
L16

1"

3/4"

2 3/4"

DRILL 23/64" DIA.
3/8" DEEP

DRILL 1/4" DIA.
1/2" DEEP

BUMPER SIDES

L17

BUMPER
L18

STEPS

L19

TOP VIEW (RIGHT-SIDE)

SIDE VIEW

L19

SHOVEL BUSHING SUPPORT

L20

DRILL 15/64" DIA.
3/4" DEEP
(AT BOTH ENDS)

L20

SIDE VIEW

ARM SIDES

L21

DRILL
17/64" DIA.

DRILL
17/64" DIA.

FRONT

ARM ASSEMBLY

L22

DRILL
17/64" DIA.

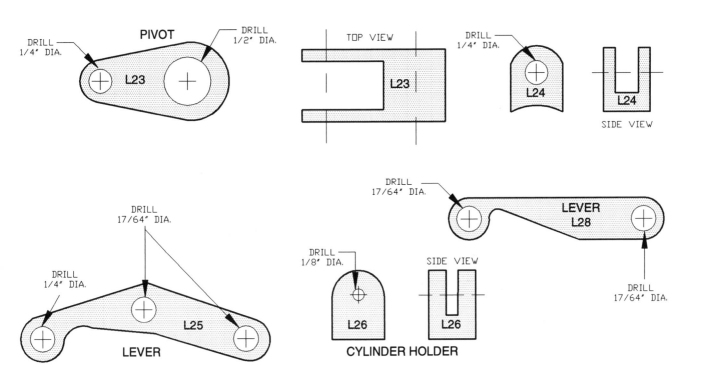

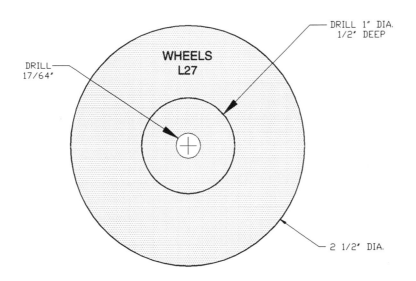

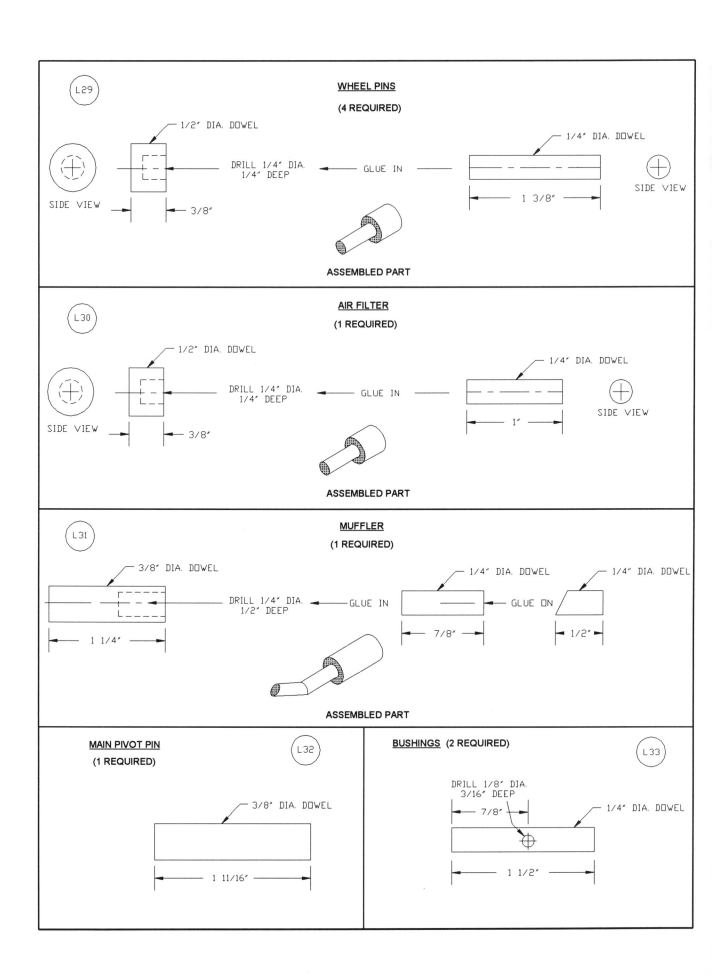

WHEEL PINS

(4 REQUIRED)

L29

1/2″ DIA. DOWEL

DRILL 1/4″ DIA. 1/4″ DEEP

GLUE IN

1/4″ DIA. DOWEL

SIDE VIEW

3/8″

1 3/8″

SIDE VIEW

ASSEMBLED PART

AIR FILTER

(1 REQUIRED)

L30

1/2″ DIA. DOWEL

DRILL 1/4″ DIA. 1/4″ DEEP

GLUE IN

1/4″ DIA. DOWEL

SIDE VIEW

3/8″

1″

SIDE VIEW

ASSEMBLED PART

MUFFLER

(1 REQUIRED)

L31

3/8″ DIA. DOWEL

DRILL 1/4″ DIA. 1/2″ DEEP

GLUE IN

1/4″ DIA. DOWEL

GLUE ON

1/4″ DIA. DOWEL

1 1/4″

7/8″

1/2″

ASSEMBLED PART

MAIN PIVOT PIN

(1 REQUIRED)

L32

3/8″ DIA. DOWEL

1 11/16″

BUSHINGS (2 REQUIRED)

L33

DRILL 1/8″ DIA. 3/16″ DEEP

7/8″

1/4″ DIA. DOWEL

1 1/2″

Loader: Pins, Shafts, Etc.

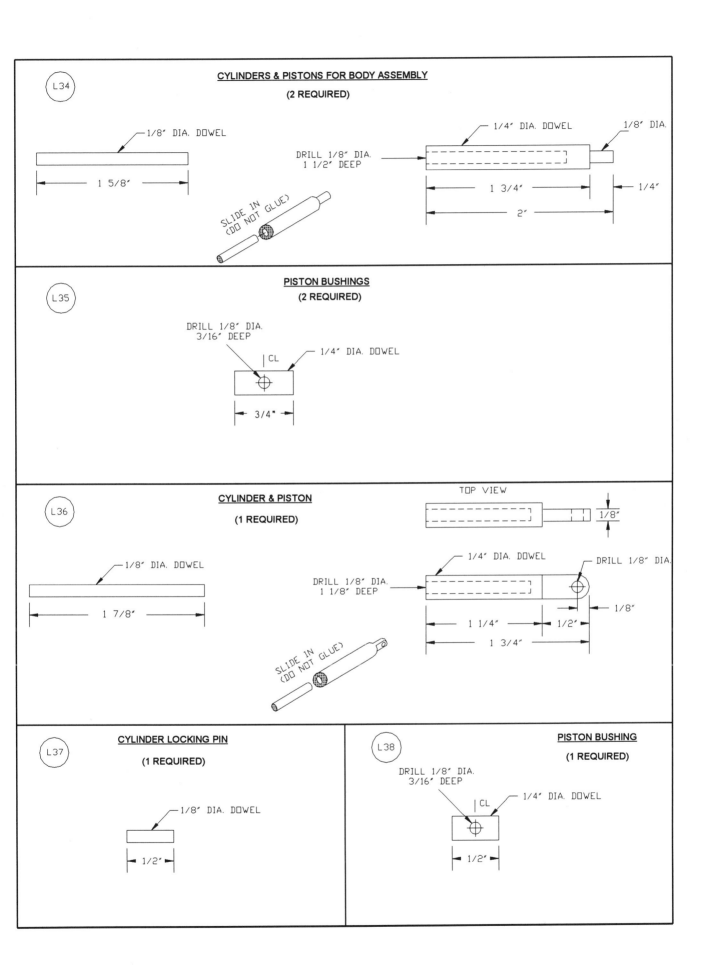

CYLINDERS & PISTONS FOR BODY ASSEMBLY

(2 REQUIRED)

L34

1/8″ DIA. DOWEL

1 5/8″

1/4″ DIA. DOWEL

1/8″ DIA.

DRILL 1/8″ DIA.
1 1/2″ DEEP

SLIDE IN
(DO NOT GLUE)

1 3/4″

1/4″

2″

PISTON BUSHINGS

(2 REQUIRED)

L35

DRILL 1/8″ DIA.
3/16″ DEEP

CL

1/4″ DIA. DOWEL

3/4″

CYLINDER & PISTON

(1 REQUIRED)

L36

TOP VIEW

1/8″

1/8″ DIA. DOWEL

1 7/8″

1/4″ DIA. DOWEL

DRILL 1/8″ DIA.
1 1/8″ DEEP

DRILL 1/8″ DIA.

1/8″

SLIDE IN
(DO NOT GLUE)

1 1/4″

1/2″

1 3/4″

CYLINDER LOCKING PIN

(1 REQUIRED)

L37

1/8″ DIA. DOWEL

1/2″

PISTON BUSHING

(1 REQUIRED)

L38

DRILL 1/8″ DIA.
3/16″ DEEP

CL

1/4″ DIA. DOWEL

1/2″

Loader: Pins, Shafts, Etc.

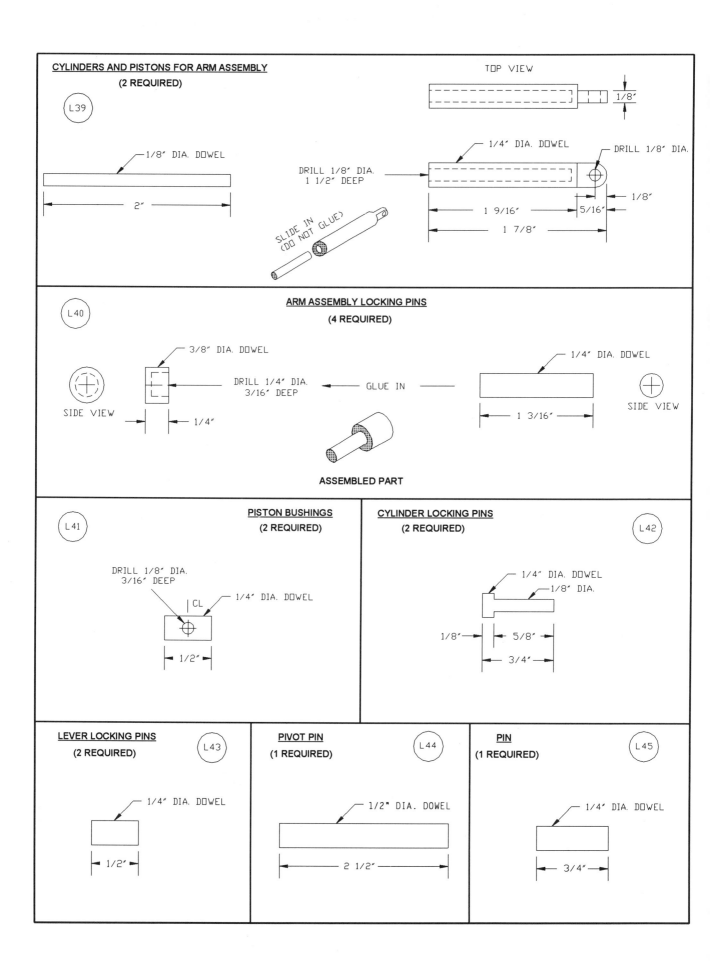

CYLINDERS AND PISTONS FOR ARM ASSEMBLY

(2 REQUIRED)

L39

TOP VIEW

1/8"

1/8" DIA. DOWEL

2"

1/4" DIA. DOWEL

DRILL 1/8" DIA.
1 1/2" DEEP

DRILL 1/8" DIA.

1/8"

1 9/16"

5/16"

1 7/8"

SLIDE IN
(DO NOT GLUE)

L40

ARM ASSEMBLY LOCKING PINS

(4 REQUIRED)

3/8" DIA. DOWEL

DRILL 1/4" DIA.
3/16" DEEP

GLUE IN

1/4" DIA. DOWEL

SIDE VIEW

1/4"

1 3/16"

SIDE VIEW

ASSEMBLED PART

L41

PISTON BUSHINGS

(2 REQUIRED)

DRILL 1/8" DIA.
3/16" DEEP

CL

1/4" DIA. DOWEL

1/2"

CYLINDER LOCKING PINS

(2 REQUIRED)

L42

1/4" DIA. DOWEL

1/8" DIA.

1/8"

5/8"

3/4"

LEVER LOCKING PINS

(2 REQUIRED)

L43

1/4" DIA. DOWEL

1/2"

PIVOT PIN

(1 REQUIRED)

L44

1/2" DIA. DOWEL

2 1/2"

PIN

(1 REQUIRED)

L45

1/4" DIA. DOWEL

3/4"

Loader: Pins, Shafts, Etc.

Glue shovel bushing support L20 to shovel assembly, as shown below.

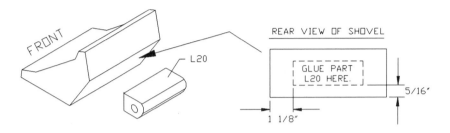

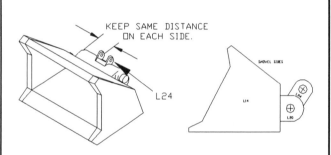

Glue part L24, as shown.

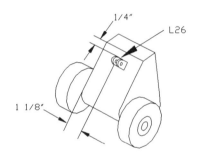

Glue part L26, as shown.

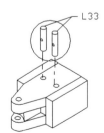 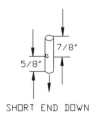

Insert bushings L33, as shown above. Make sure to insert them with the short end going in first. Do not glue.

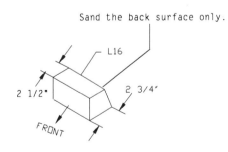

Sand an angle on the back of part L16, as shown.

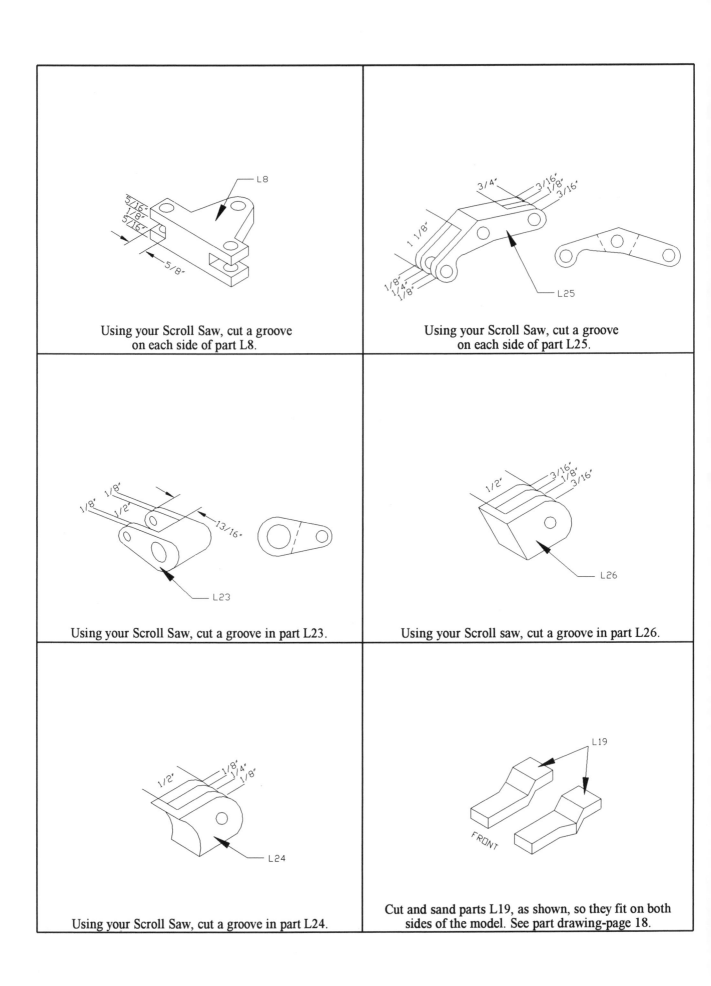

Using your Scroll Saw, cut a groove
on each side of part L8.

Using your Scroll Saw, cut a groove
on each side of part L25.

Using your Scroll Saw, cut a groove in part L23.

Using your Scroll saw, cut a groove in part L26.

Using your Scroll Saw, cut a groove in part L24.

Cut and sand parts L19, as shown, so they fit on both
sides of the model. See part drawing-page 18.

Loader - Assembly Drawings

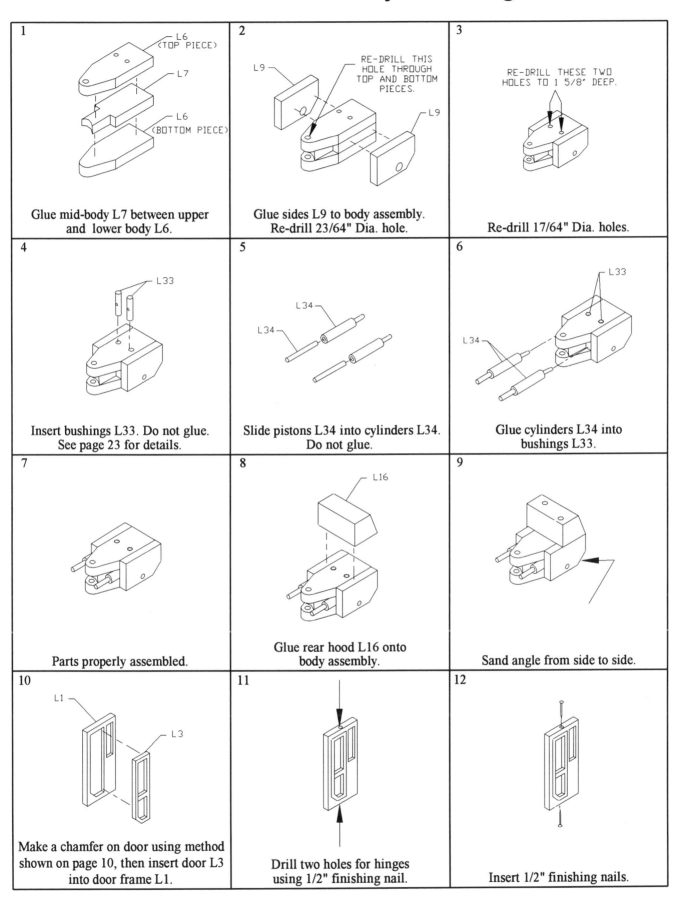

1
Glue mid-body L7 between upper and lower body L6.

2
Glue sides L9 to body assembly. Re-drill 23/64" Dia. hole.

3
Re-drill 17/64" Dia. holes.

4
Insert bushings L33. Do not glue. See page 23 for details.

5
Slide pistons L34 into cylinders L34. Do not glue.

6
Glue cylinders L34 into bushings L33.

7
Parts properly assembled.

8
Glue rear hood L16 onto body assembly.

9
Sand angle from side to side.

10
Make a chamfer on door using method shown on page 10, then insert door L3 into door frame L1.

11
Drill two holes for hinges using 1/2" finishing nail.

12
Insert 1/2" finishing nails.

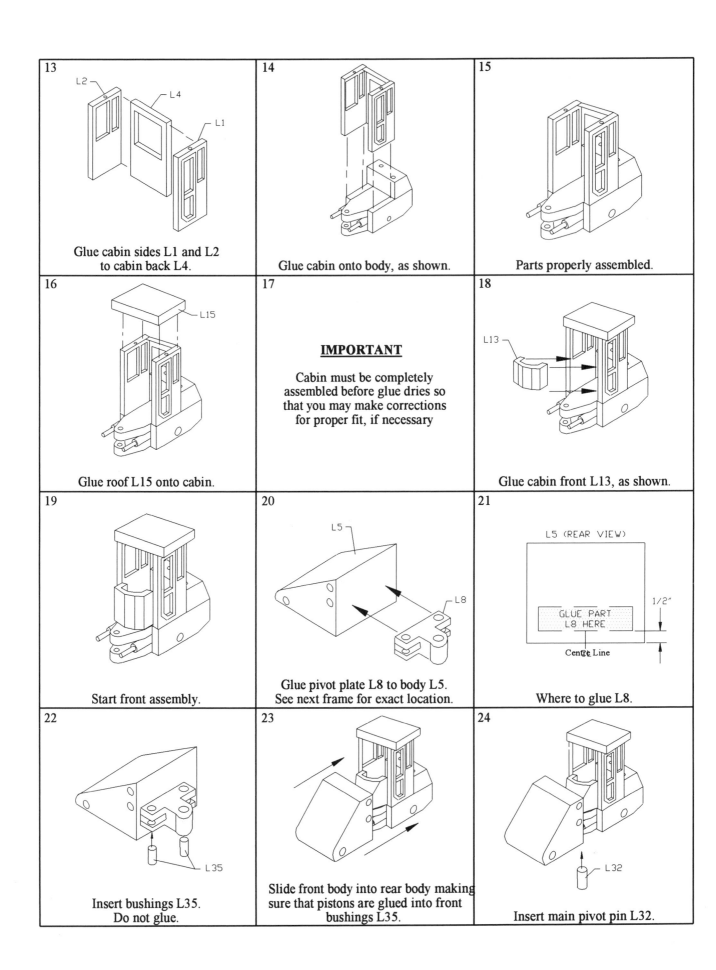

13 Glue cabin sides L1 and L2 to cabin back L4.

14 Glue cabin onto body, as shown.

15 Parts properly assembled.

16 Glue roof L15 onto cabin.

17

IMPORTANT

Cabin must be completely assembled before glue dries so that you may make corrections for proper fit, if necessary

18 Glue cabin front L13, as shown.

19 Start front assembly.

20 Glue pivot plate L8 to body L5. See next frame for exact location.

21 L5 (REAR VIEW) — GLUE PART L8 HERE — 1/2" — Centre Line — Where to glue L8.

22 Insert bushings L35. Do not glue.

23 Slide front body into rear body making sure that pistons are glued into front bushings L35.

24 Insert main pivot pin L32.

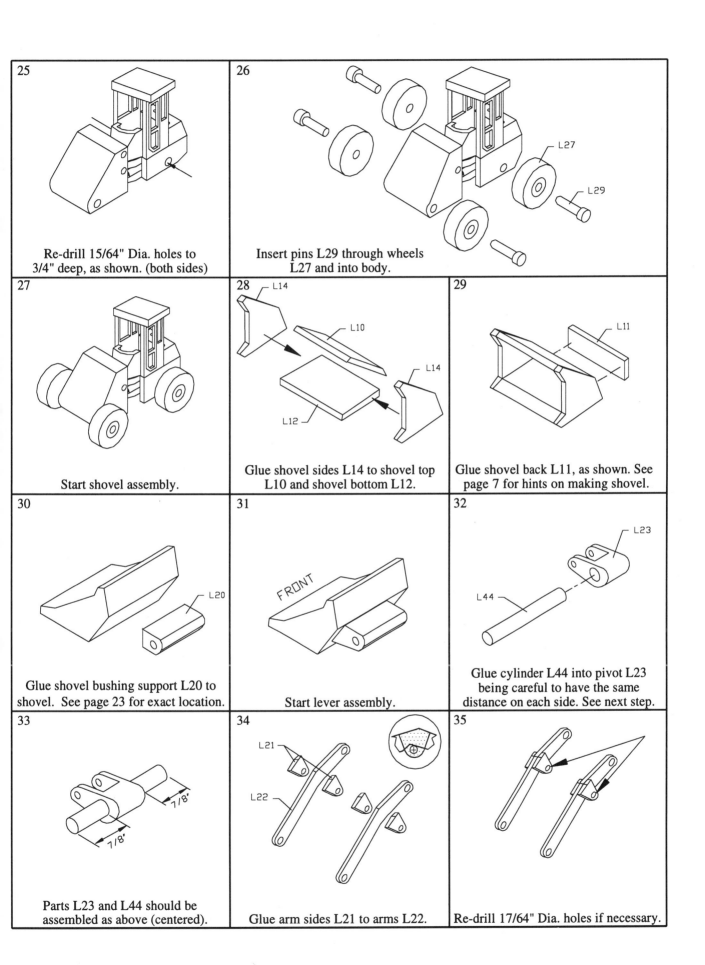

25 Re-drill 15/64" Dia. holes to 3/4" deep, as shown. (both sides)

26 Insert pins L29 through wheels L27 and into body.

L27

L29

27 Start shovel assembly.

28 L14

L10

L14

L12

Glue shovel sides L14 to shovel top L10 and shovel bottom L12.

29 L11

Glue shovel back L11, as shown. See page 7 for hints on making shovel.

30 L20

Glue shovel bushing support L20 to shovel. See page 23 for exact location.

31 FRONT

Start lever assembly.

32 L23

L44

Glue cylinder L44 into pivot L23 being careful to have the same distance on each side. See next step.

33 7/8"

7/8"

Parts L23 and L44 should be assembled as above (centered).

34 L21

L22

Glue arm sides L21 to arms L22.

35 Re-drill 17/64" Dia. holes if necessary.

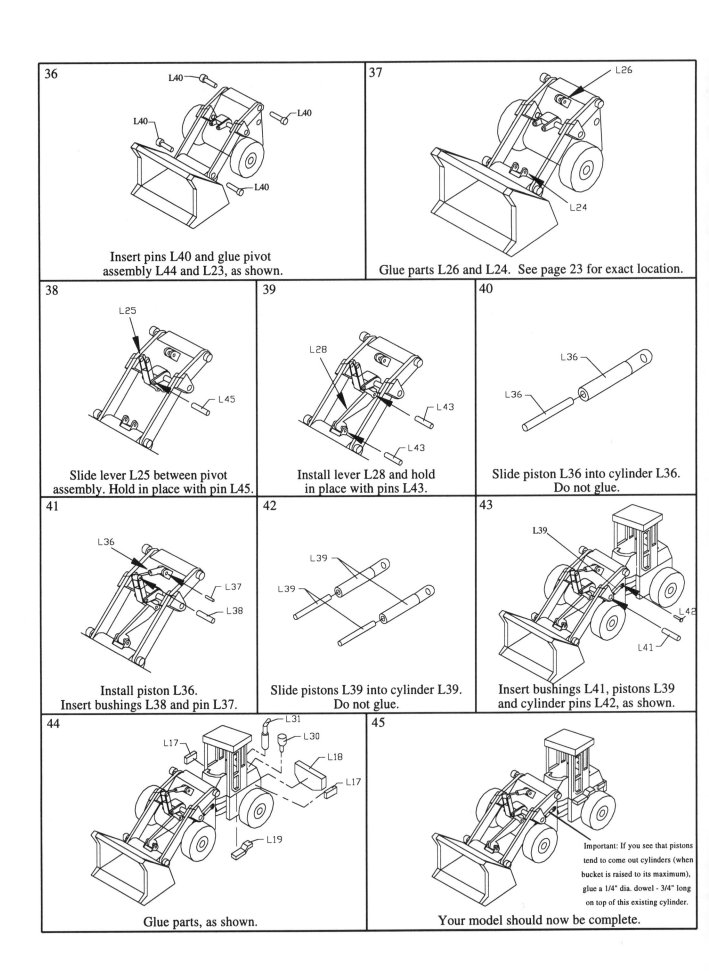

36

Insert pins L40 and glue pivot assembly L44 and L23, as shown.

37

Glue parts L26 and L24. See page 23 for exact location.

38

Slide lever L25 between pivot assembly. Hold in place with pin L45.

39

Install lever L28 and hold in place with pins L43.

40

Slide piston L36 into cylinder L36. Do not glue.

41

Install piston L36. Insert bushings L38 and pin L37.

42

Slide pistons L39 into cylinder L39. Do not glue.

43

Insert bushings L41, pistons L39 and cylinder pins L42, as shown.

44

Glue parts, as shown.

45

Important: If you see that pistons tend to come out cylinders (when bucket is raised to its maximum), glue a 1/4" dia. dowel - 3/4" long on top of this existing cylinder.

Your model should now be complete.

Loader: Assembly Drawings

DOZER

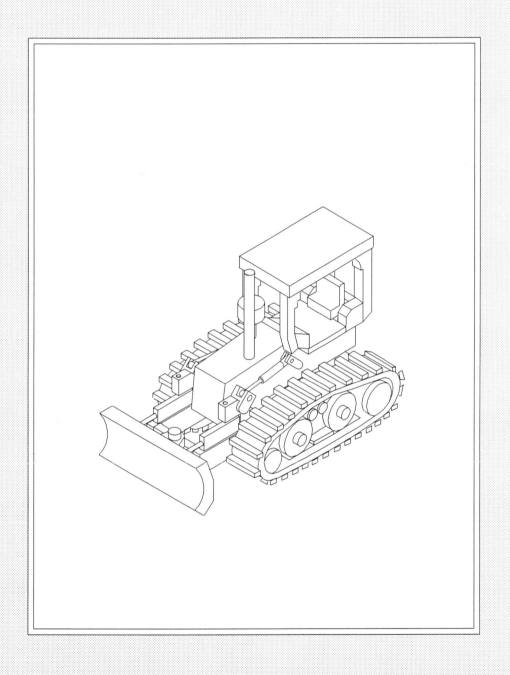

General Instructions - Dozer

1- Start by cutting materials needed by following the list of materials, paying attention to the rough and finished size. **Identify the parts as they are cut.**

   Please note: Different types of wood can be used for the various parts. It is suggested, however, that hard wood be used, since many of the parts would be much too fragile if using soft wood. We have used a combination of pine, maple and oak to give the models a nice contrast!

2- Remove the full-size patterns found in the appendix. Cut them out, leaving approximately 1/16" all around, and place on the proper piece of wood. Patterns can be secured to wood using either spray adhesive or rubber ciment. If using the latter, cut and sand the part first to finished size. If drilling is required, mark the hole by inserting a scriber or nail through the pattern into the wood. Remove the pattern before drilling.

   You should have no trouble determining which surface to attach most of the patterns. Some parts, however, can be confusing since the pattern could fit on more than one surface. The drawings below indicate exactly which surface to attach the patterns for these parts.

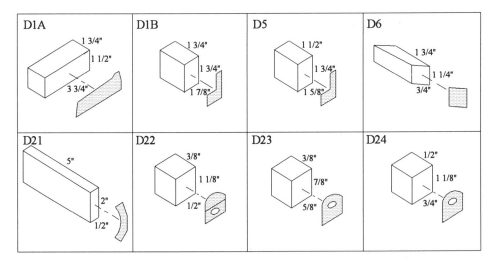

3- Look at the full-size drawing sheets to finish parts D3, D16, and D19.

4- Parts D1A, D17, D18, D20, D22, D23 and D24 will need additional cuts and details, please refer to the additional information pages, to complete these parts.

5- Using maple dowels, make all pins, shafts, etc.

6- Follow the assembly drawings to complete your model.

List of Materials - Dozer

Part	T	W	L	Material	Qty.	*
D1	1"	1 3/4"	6 13/16"	pine	1	F
D1A	1 1/2"	1 3/4"	3 3/4"	pine	1	F
D1B	1 3/4"	1 3/4"	1 7/8"	pine	1	F
D2	3/8"	2 3/4"	1 7/16"	pine	1	F
D3	1/2"	1 1/2"	1 3/4"	oak	2	F
D4	1/4"	2 3/4"	3 3/4"	pine	1	F
D5	1 1/2"	1 3/4"	1 5/8"	pine	1	R
D6	3/4"	1 3/4"	1 1/4"	oak	1	F
D7	3/8"	1 1/4"	3 1/2"	oak	2	R
D8	3/8"	1 1/4"	3 1/2"	oak	2	R
D9	1/8"	1/4"	1 3/8"	pine	72	F
D10	1/4"	3/8"	1"	pine	6	F
D11	1/4"	1 3/8" DIA.		maple	4	F
D12	1/4"	1/2" DIA.		maple	4	F

Part	T	W	L	Material	Qty.	*
D13	1/4"	1 1/4" DIA.		maple	4	F
D14	1 1/4"	2"	7"	pine	2	F
D15	1/4"	1/2"	3 3/4"	pine	2	F
D15A	1/4"	1/2"	3 3/4"	pine	2	F
D16	3/4"	3 1/4"	5 3/4"	pine	1	F
D17	1/4"	2"	2 1/2"	maple	2	R
D18	1/4"	3/8"	1 3/8"	maple	2	F
D19	5/8"	1/2"	1 3/4"	maple	1	F
D20	1/2"	1 5/8"	2 3/4"	maple	1	R
D21	1/2"	2"	5"	pine	1	F
D22	3/8"	1/2"	1 1/8"	maple	2	R
D23	3/8"	5/8"	7/8"	maple	2	R
D24	1/2"	3/4"	1 1/8"	maple	1	R

T = Thickness
W = Width
L = Length

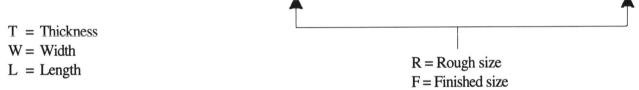

R = Rough size
F = Finished size

Instructions:

R= Rough sizes, the material is cut oversized so you have ample room to apply the pattern on the surface. Sanding is not required at this point.

F = Finished Size: Cut and sand parts to finished size.

Full-Sized Patterns: Set One

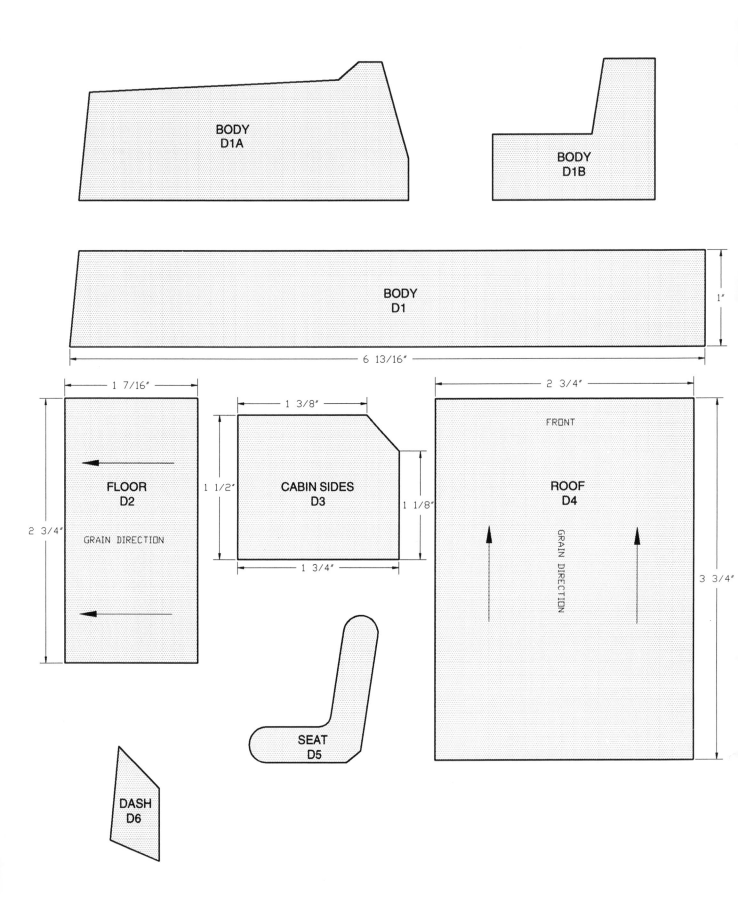

BODY
D1A

BODY
D1B

BODY
D1

1″

6 13/16″

1 7/16″

FLOOR
D2

GRAIN DIRECTION

2 3/4″

1 3/8″

1 1/2″

CABIN SIDES
D3

1 1/8″

1 3/4″

2 3/4″

FRONT

ROOF
D4

GRAIN DIRECTION

3 3/4″

SEAT
D5

DASH
D6

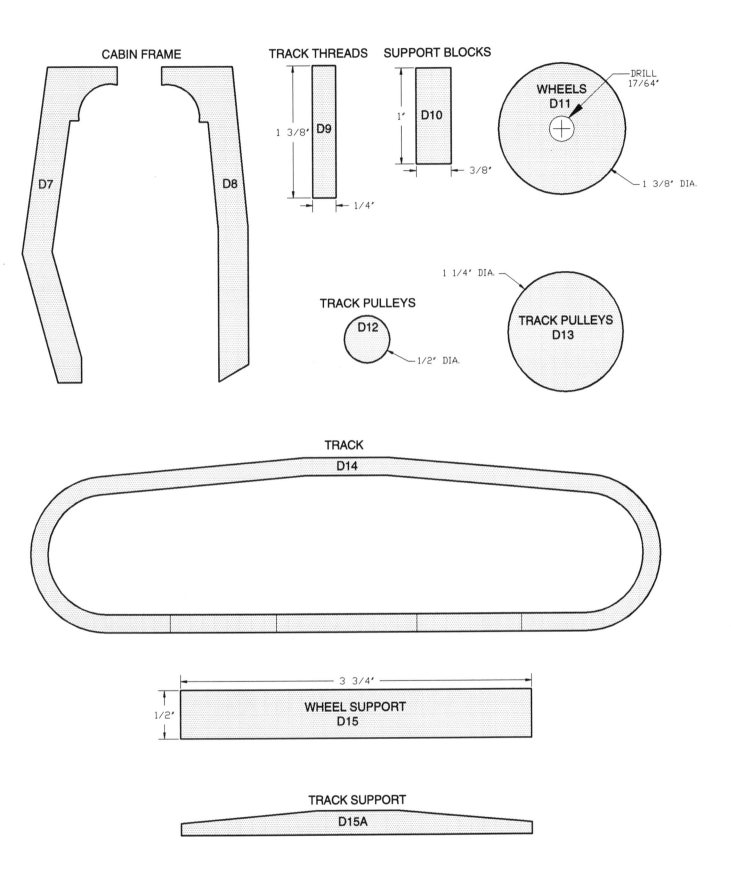

CABIN FRAME

D7

D8

TRACK THREADS

D9

1 3/8'

1/4"

SUPPORT BLOCKS

D10

1"

3/8"

WHEELS
D11

DRILL
17/64'

1 3/8' DIA.

TRACK PULLEYS

D12

1/2' DIA.

1 1/4' DIA.

TRACK PULLEYS
D13

TRACK
D14

WHEEL SUPPORT
D15

3 3/4'

1/2'

TRACK SUPPORT

D15A

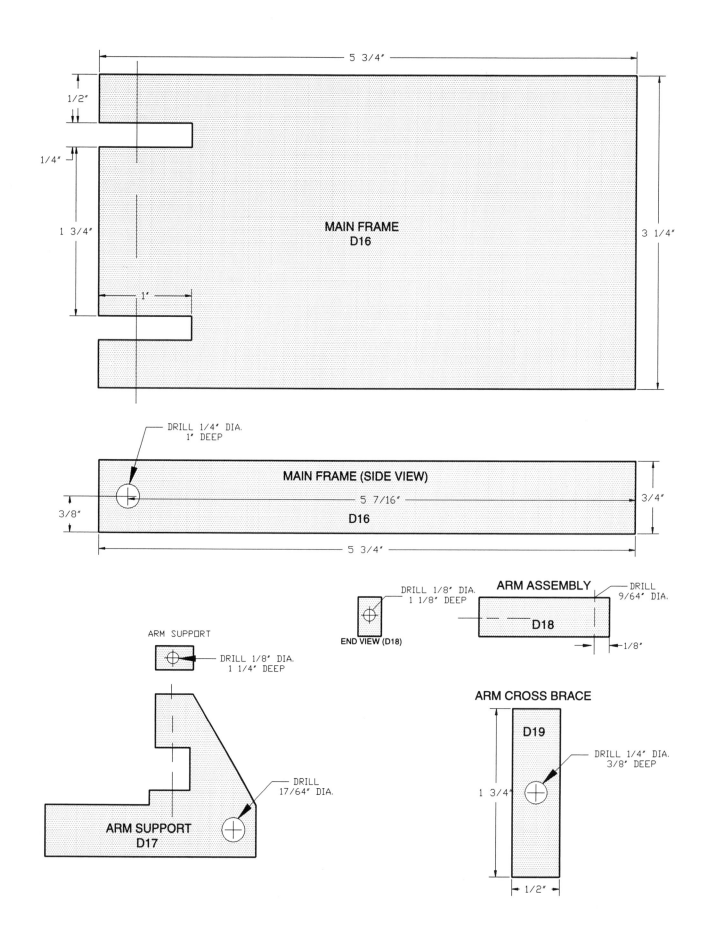

MAIN FRAME
D16

5 3/4"

1/2"

1/4"

1 3/4"

1"

3 1/4"

DRILL 1/4" DIA.
1" DEEP

MAIN FRAME (SIDE VIEW)

5 7/16"

D16

3/4"

3/8"

5 3/4"

ARM SUPPORT

DRILL 1/8" DIA.
1 1/4" DEEP

ARM SUPPORT
D17

DRILL
17/64" DIA.

DRILL 1/8" DIA.
1 1/8" DEEP

END VIEW (D18)

ARM ASSEMBLY

DRILL
9/64" DIA.

D18

1/8"

ARM CROSS BRACE

D19

1 3/4"

DRILL 1/4" DIA.
3/8" DEEP

1/2"

PIVOT ASSEMBLY

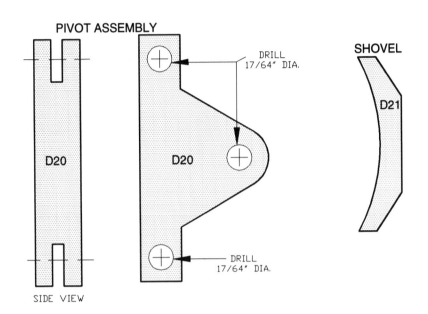

D20

SIDE VIEW

D20

DRILL
17/64" DIA.

DRILL
17/64" DIA.

SHOVEL

D21

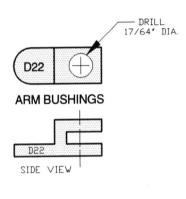

DRILL
17/64" DIA.

D22

ARM BUSHINGS

D22

SIDE VIEW

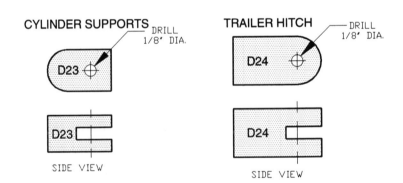

CYLINDER SUPPORTS

DRILL
1/8" DIA.

D23

D23

SIDE VIEW

TRAILER HITCH

DRILL
1/8" DIA.

D24

D24

SIDE VIEW

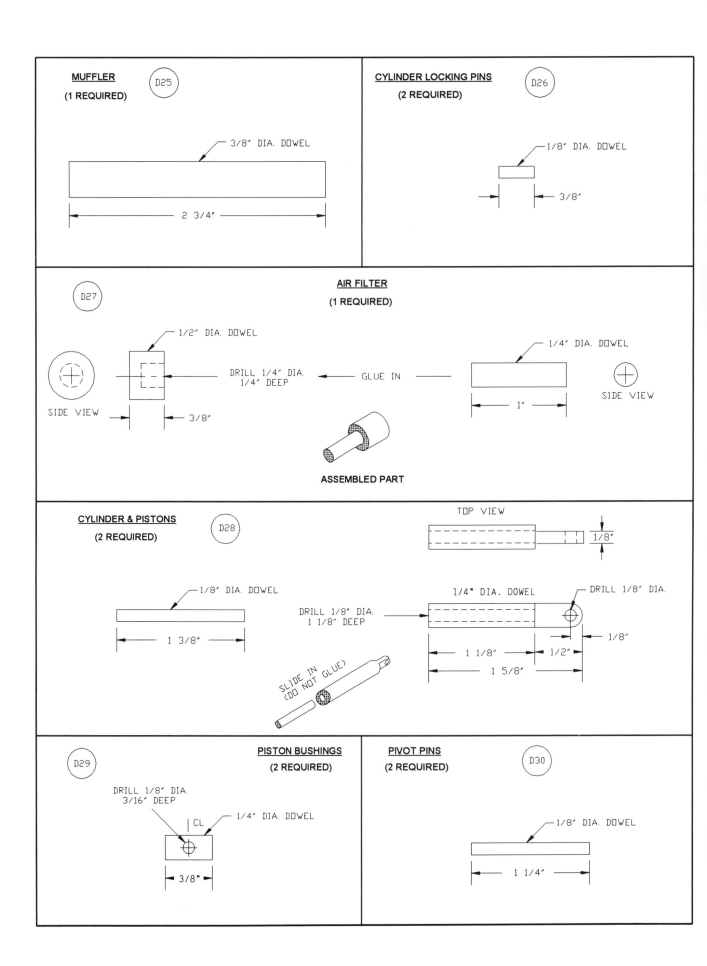

MUFFLER
(1 REQUIRED)

D25

3/8″ DIA. DOWEL

2 3/4″

CYLINDER LOCKING PINS
(2 REQUIRED)

D26

1/8″ DIA. DOWEL

3/8″

AIR FILTER
(1 REQUIRED)

D27

1/2″ DIA. DOWEL

DRILL 1/4″ DIA.
1/4″ DEEP

GLUE IN

1/4″ DIA. DOWEL

SIDE VIEW

SIDE VIEW

3/8″

1″

ASSEMBLED PART

CYLINDER & PISTONS
(2 REQUIRED)

D28

TOP VIEW

1/8″

1/8″ DIA. DOWEL

1 3/8″

DRILL 1/8″ DIA.
1 1/8″ DEEP

SLIDE IN
(DO NOT GLUE)

1/4" DIA. DOWEL

DRILL 1/8″ DIA.

1/8″

1 1/8″   1/2″

1 5/8″

PISTON BUSHINGS
(2 REQUIRED)

D29

DRILL 1/8″ DIA.
3/16″ DEEP

CL

1/4″ DIA. DOWEL

3/8"

PIVOT PINS
(2 REQUIRED)

D30

1/8″ DIA. DOWEL

1 1/4″

Dozer: Pins, Shafts, Etc.

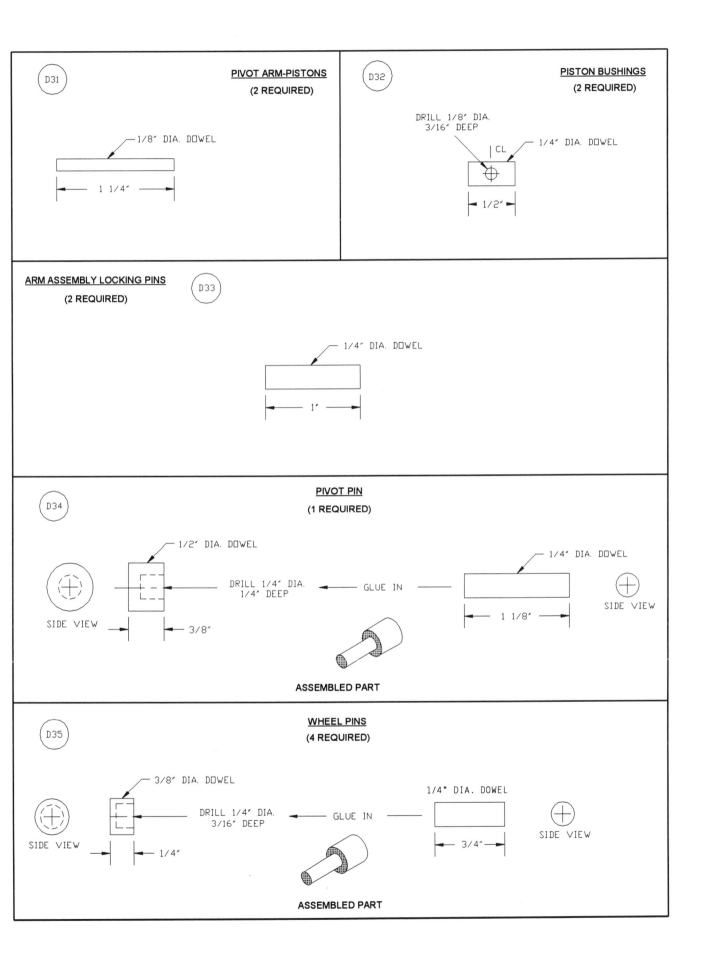

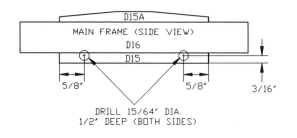

Drill holes into frame assembly, as shown.

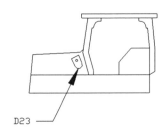

Glue parts D23 on each side of model.

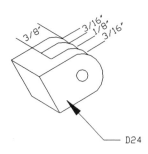

Using your Scroll Saw, cut a groove in part D24.

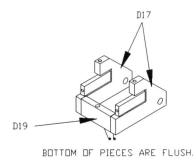

BOTTOM OF PIECES ARE FLUSH.

Glue part D19 between parts D17
keeping bottom of parts flush.

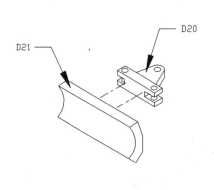

Glue part D20 in the middle (centered) of part D21.

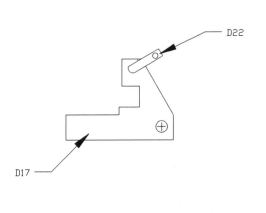

Glue parts D22 onto D17, as shown.

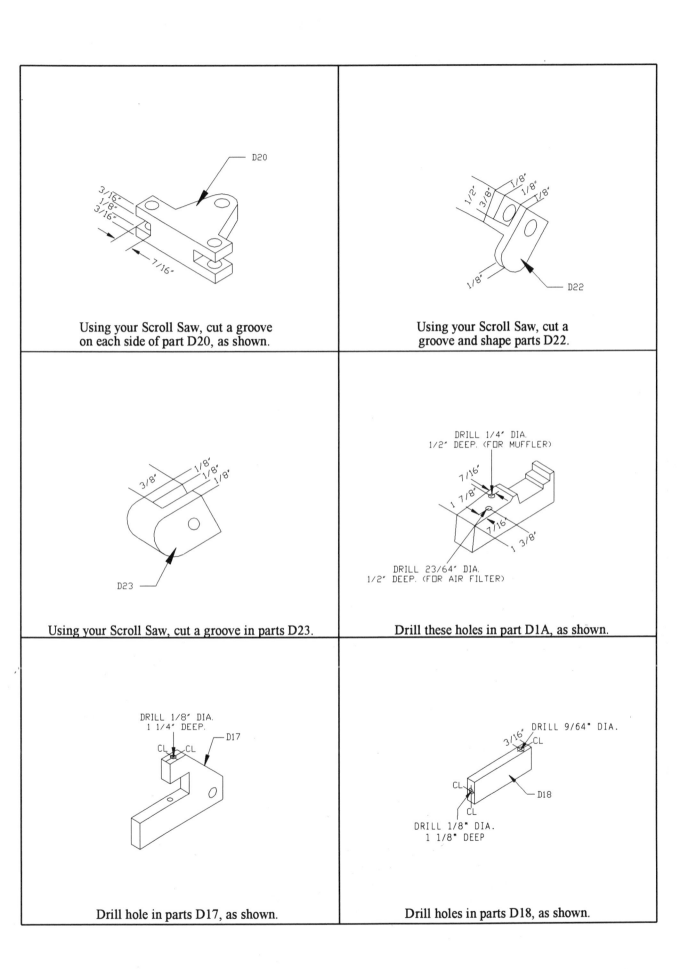

Using your Scroll Saw, cut a groove
on each side of part D20, as shown.

Using your Scroll Saw, cut a
groove and shape parts D22.

Using your Scroll Saw, cut a groove in parts D23.

Drill these holes in part D1A, as shown.

Drill hole in parts D17, as shown.

Drill holes in parts D18, as shown.

Dozer - Assembly Drawings

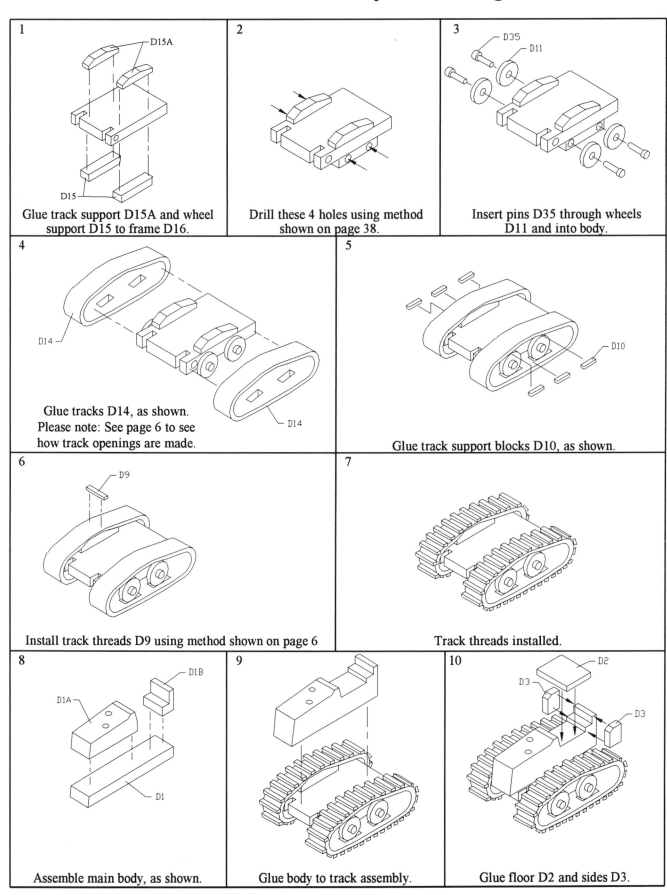

1 Glue track support D15A and wheel support D15 to frame D16.

2 Drill these 4 holes using method shown on page 38.

3 Insert pins D35 through wheels D11 and into body.

4 Glue tracks D14, as shown. Please note: See page 6 to see how track openings are made.

5 Glue track support blocks D10, as shown.

6 Install track threads D9 using method shown on page 6

7 Track threads installed.

8 Assemble main body, as shown.

9 Glue body to track assembly.

10 Glue floor D2 and sides D3.

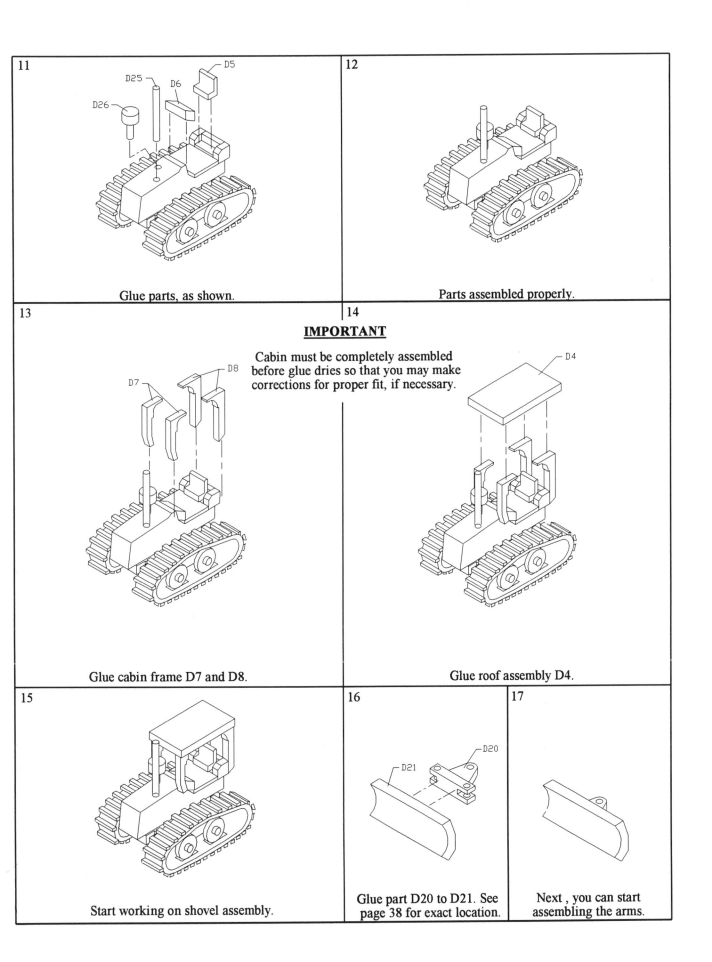

11

D26 D25 D6 D5

Glue parts, as shown.

12

Parts assembled properly.

13

D7 D8

Glue cabin frame D7 and D8.

14

IMPORTANT

Cabin must be completely assembled
before glue dries so that you may make
corrections for proper fit, if necessary.

D4

Glue roof assembly D4.

15

Start working on shovel assembly.

16

D20 D21

Glue part D20 to D21. See
page 38 for exact location.

17

Next , you can start
assembling the arms.

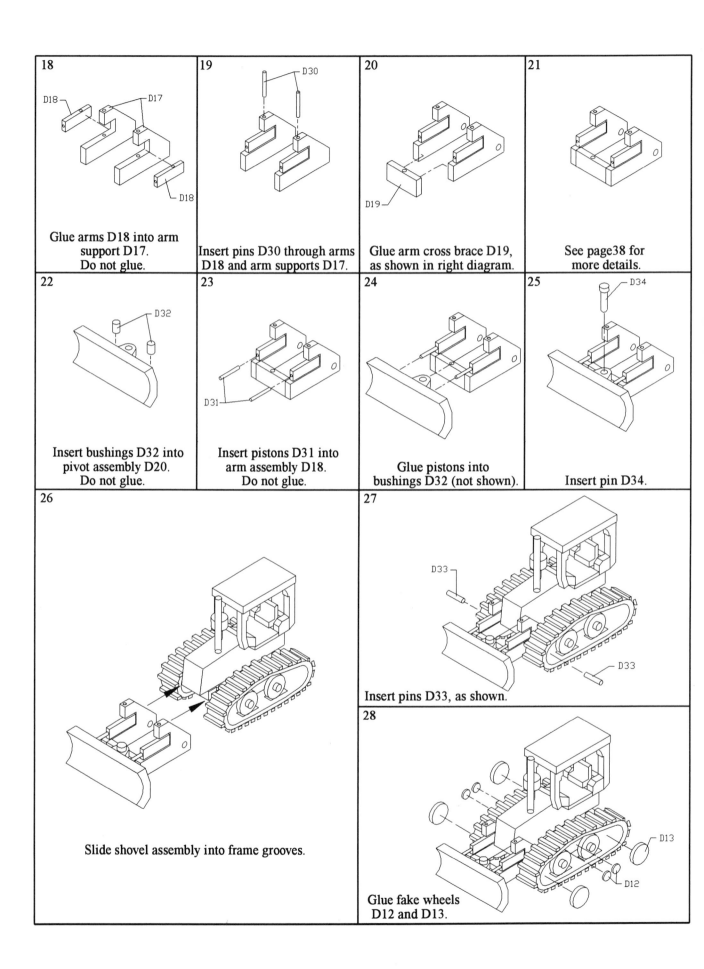

18

Glue arms D18 into arm
support D17.
Do not glue.

19

Insert pins D30 through arms
D18 and arm supports D17.

20

Glue arm cross brace D19,
as shown in right diagram.

21

See page38 for
more details.

22

Insert bushings D32 into
pivot assembly D20.
Do not glue.

23

Insert pistons D31 into
arm assembly D18.
Do not glue.

24

Glue pistons into
bushings D32 (not shown).

25

Insert pin D34.

26

Slide shovel assembly into frame grooves.

27

Insert pins D33, as shown.

28

Glue fake wheels
D12 and D13.

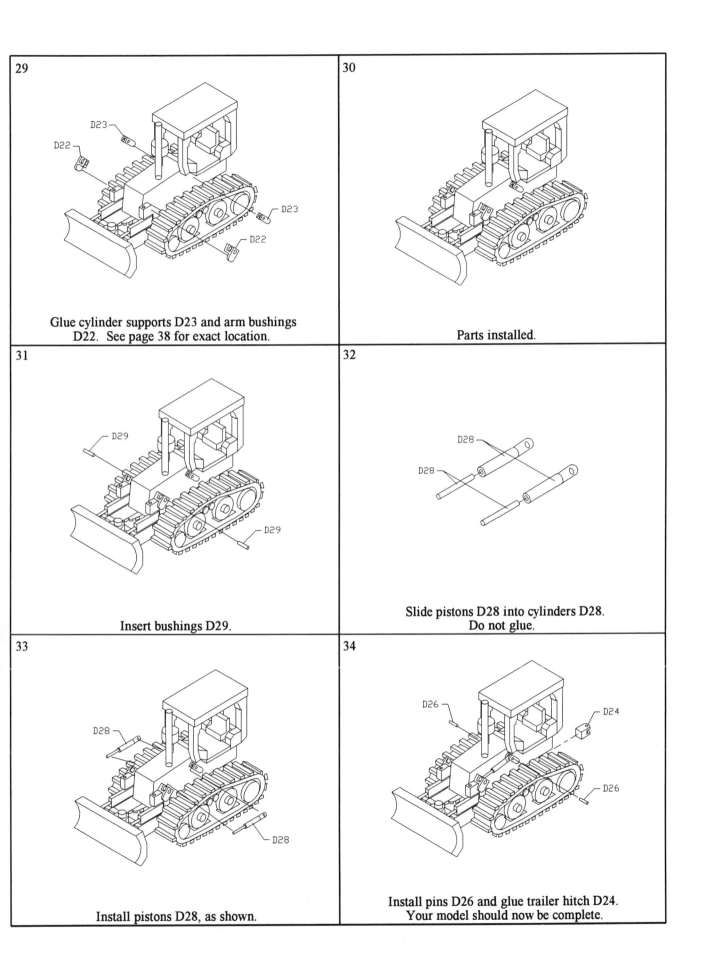

29

Glue cylinder supports D23 and arm bushings D22. See page 38 for exact location.

30

Parts installed.

31

Insert bushings D29.

32

Slide pistons D28 into cylinders D28. Do not glue.

33

Install pistons D28, as shown.

34

Install pins D26 and glue trailer hitch D24. Your model should now be complete.

DOZER LOADER

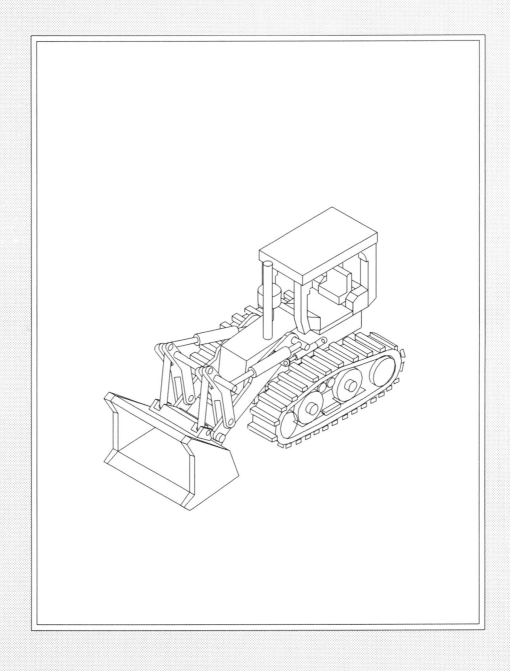

General Instructions - Dozer Loader

1- Start by cutting materials needed by following the list of materials, paying attention to the rough and finished size. **Identify the parts as they are cut.**

   Please note: Different types of wood can be used for the various parts. It is suggested, however, that hard wood be used, since many of the parts would be much too fragile if using soft wood. We have used a combination of pine, maple and oak to give the models a nice contrast!

2- Remove the full-size patterns found in the appendix. Cut them out, leaving approximately 1/16" all around, and place on the proper piece of wood. Patterns can be secured to wood using either spray adhesive or rubber ciment. If using the latter, cut and sand the part first to finished size. If drilling is required, mark the hole by inserting a scriber or nail through the pattern into the wood. Remove the pattern before drilling.

   You should have no trouble determining which surface to attach most of the patterns. Some parts, however, can be confusing since the pattern could fit on more than one surface. The drawings below indicate exactly which surface to attach the patterns for these parts.

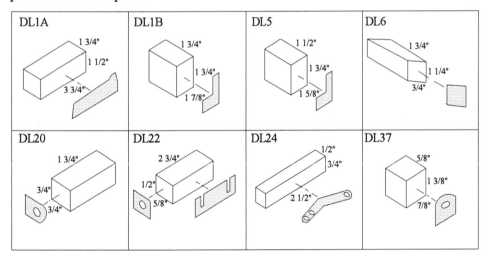

3- Look at the full-size drawing sheets to finish parts DL1, and DL3.

4- Parts DL1A, DL21, DL22, DL24, and DL37 will need additional cuts and details, please refer to the additional information pages, to complete these parts.

5- Using maple dowels, make all pins, shafts, etc.

6- Follow the assembly drawings to complete your model.

List of Materials - Dozer Loader

Part	T	W	L	Material	Qty.	*
DL1	1"	1 3/4"	6 13/16"	pine	1	F
DL1A	1 1/2"	1 3/4"	3 3/4"	pine	1	R
DL1B	1 3/4"	1 3/4"	1 7/8"	pine	1	F
DL2	3/8"	2 3/4"	1 7/16"	pine	1	F
DL3	1/2"	1 1/2"	1 3/4"	oak	2	F
DL4	1/4"	2 3/4"	3 3/4"	pine	1	F
DL5	1 1/2"	1 3/4"	1 5/8"	pine	1	R
DL6	3/4"	1 3/4"	1 1/4"	oak	1	R
DL7	3/8"	1 1/4"	3 1/2"	oak	2	R
DL8	3/8"	1 1/4"	3 1/2"	oak	2	R
DL9	1/8"	1/4"	1 3/8"	pine	72	F
DL10	1/4"	3/8"	1"	pine	6	F
DL11	1/4"	1 3/8" DIA.		maple	4	F
DL12	1/4"	1/2" DIA.		maple	4	F
DL13	1/4"	1 1/4" DIA.		maple	4	F

Part	T	W	L	Material	Qty.	*
DL14	1 1/4"	2"	7"	pine	2	R
DL15	1/4"	1/2"	3 3/4"	pine	2	F
DL15a	1/4"	1/2"	3 3/4"	pine	2	F
DL16	1/4"	2 3/4"	4 1/2"	pine	1	F
DL17	1/8"	1 5/8"	5"	pine	1	F
DL18	1/4"	1 7/8"	4 1/2"	pine	1	F
DL19	1/4"	2 7/8"	2 7/8"	pine	2	R
DL20	3/4"	3/4"	1 3/4"	maple	1	F
DL21	3/8"	3/4"	1 1/4"	maple	2	R
DL22	1/2"	5/8"	2 1/2"	maple	1	F
DL23	1/4"	1"	4 3/4"	maple	2	R
DL24	1/2"	3/4"	2 1/2"	maple	2	R
DL37	5/8"	7/8"	1 3/8"	Maple	1	R
DL38	3/4"	3 1/4"	5 3/4"	pine	1	F

T = Thickness
W = Width
L = Length

R = Rough size
F = Finished size

Instructions:

R= Rough sizes, the material is cut oversized so you have ample room to apply the pattern on the surface. Sanding is not required at this point.

F = Finished Size: Cut and sand parts to finished size.

Full-Sized Patterns: Set One

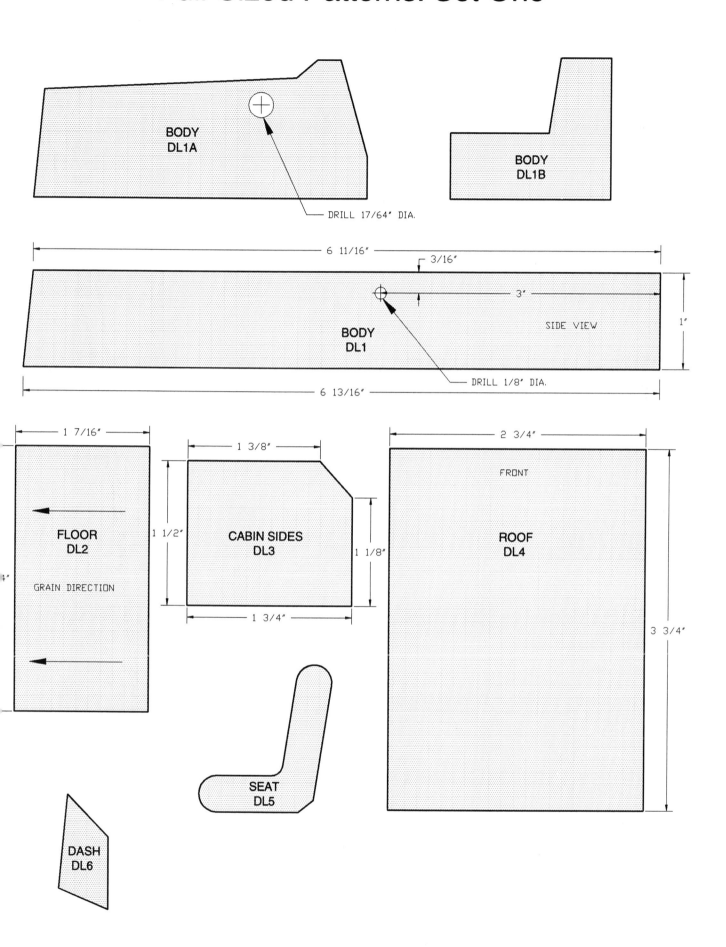

BODY
DL1A

DRILL 17/64" DIA.

BODY
DL1B

6 11/16"

3/16"

3"

SIDE VIEW

1"

BODY
DL1

DRILL 1/8" DIA.

6 13/16"

1 7/16"

FLOOR
DL2

GRAIN DIRECTION

4"

1 3/8"

1 1/2"

CABIN SIDES
DL3

1 1/8"

1 3/4"

2 3/4"

FRONT

ROOF
DL4

3 3/4"

SEAT
DL5

DASH
DL6

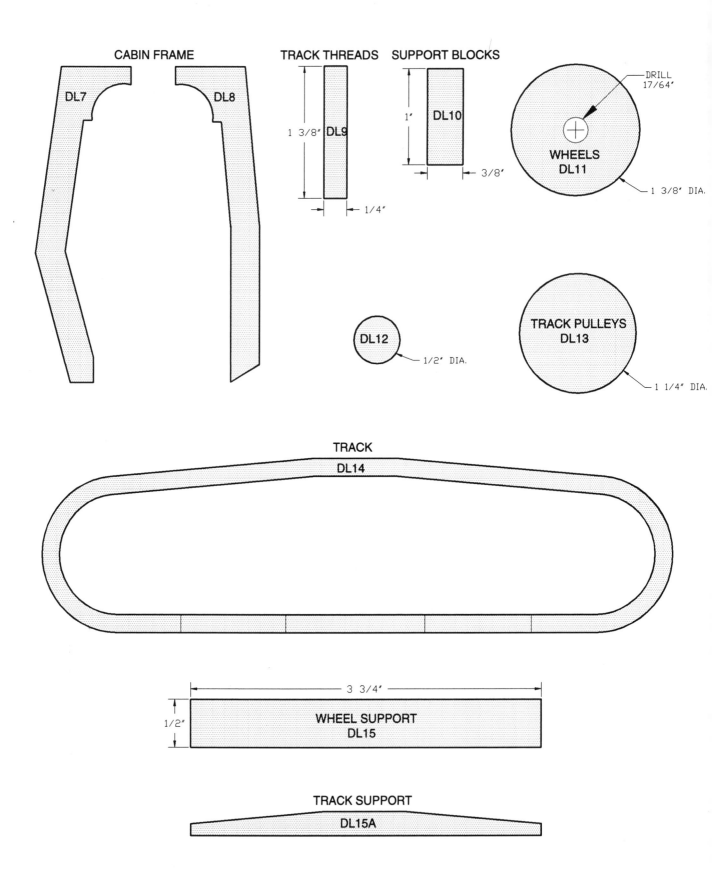

CABIN FRAME

DL7

DL8

TRACK THREADS

1 3/8"   DL9

1/4"

SUPPORT BLOCKS

1'   DL10

3/8"

WHEELS
DL11

DRILL
17/64"

1 3/8" DIA.

DL12

1/2" DIA.

TRACK PULLEYS
DL13

1 1/4" DIA.

TRACK
DL14

3 3/4"

1/2"

WHEEL SUPPORT
DL15

TRACK SUPPORT
DL15A

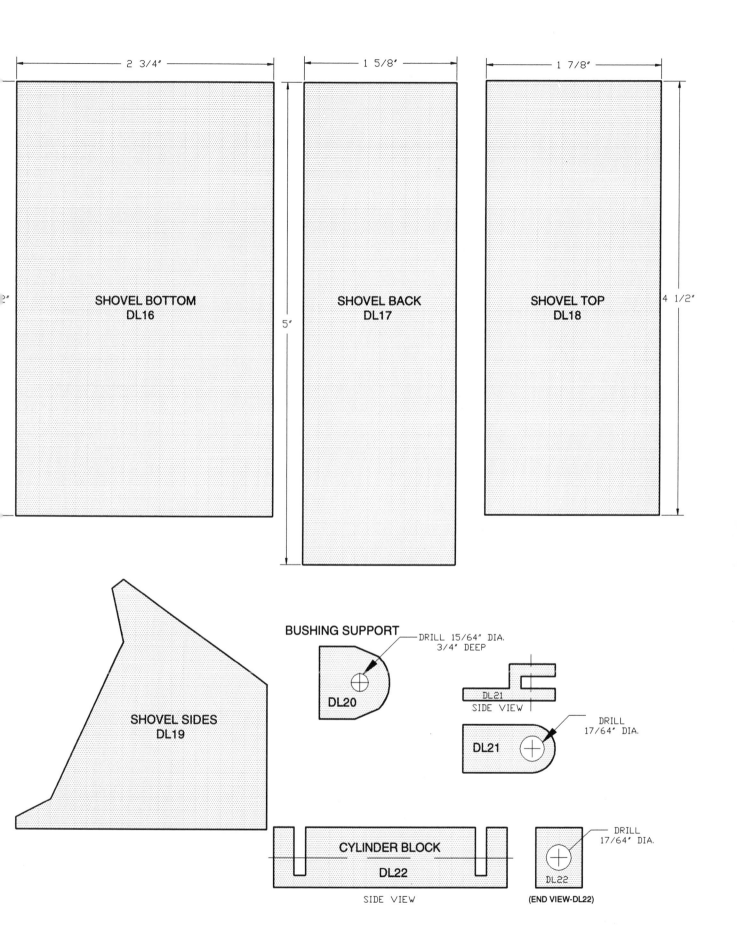

2 3/4"

1 5/8"

1 7/8"

SHOVEL BOTTOM
DL16

SHOVEL BACK
DL17

SHOVEL TOP
DL18

5"

4 1/2"

SHOVEL SIDES
DL19

BUSHING SUPPORT

DRILL 15/64" DIA.
3/4" DEEP

DL20

DL21
SIDE VIEW

DRILL
17/64" DIA.

DL21

CYLINDER BLOCK

DL22

SIDE VIEW

DRILL
17/64" DIA.

DL22

(END VIEW-DL22)

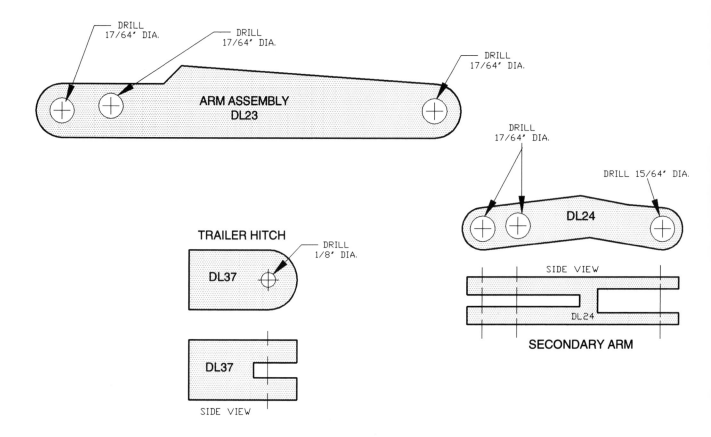

DRILL
17/64" DIA.

DRILL
17/64" DIA.

DRILL
17/64" DIA.

ARM ASSEMBLY
DL23

DRILL
17/64" DIA.

DRILL 15/64" DIA.

DL24

TRAILER HITCH

DRILL
1/8" DIA.

DL37

SIDE VIEW

DL24

SECONDARY ARM

DL37

SIDE VIEW

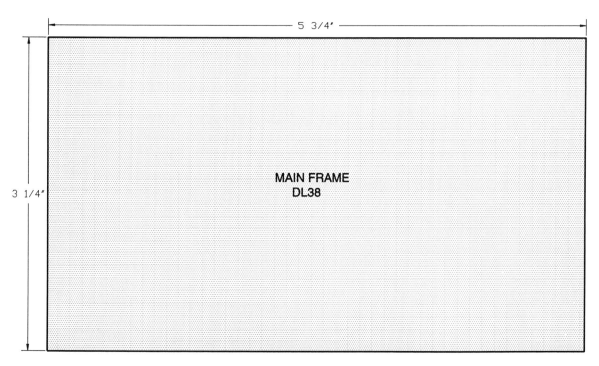

5 3/4"

3 1/4"

MAIN FRAME
DL38

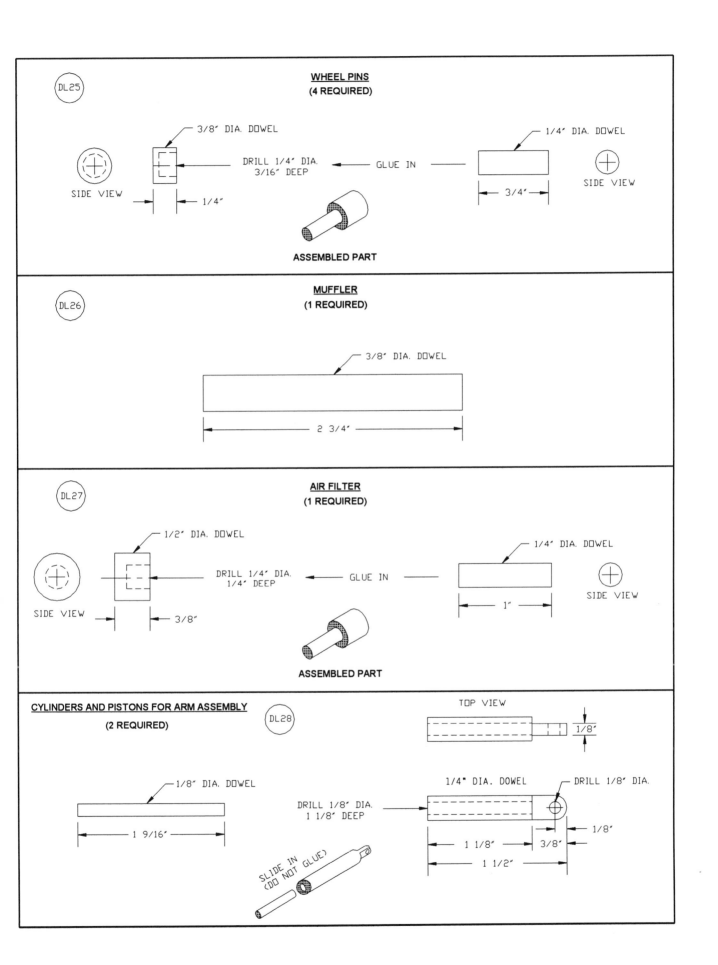

WHEEL PINS
(4 REQUIRED)

DL25

SIDE VIEW

3/8″ DIA. DOWEL

DRILL 1/4″ DIA.
3/16″ DEEP

GLUE IN

1/4″ DIA. DOWEL

SIDE VIEW

3/4″

1/4″

ASSEMBLED PART

MUFFLER
(1 REQUIRED)

DL26

3/8″ DIA. DOWEL

2 3/4″

AIR FILTER
(1 REQUIRED)

DL27

SIDE VIEW

1/2″ DIA. DOWEL

DRILL 1/4″ DIA.
1/4″ DEEP

GLUE IN

1/4″ DIA. DOWEL

SIDE VIEW

3/8″

1″

ASSEMBLED PART

CYLINDERS AND PISTONS FOR ARM ASSEMBLY
(2 REQUIRED)

DL28

TOP VIEW

1/8″

1/8″ DIA. DOWEL

1 9/16″

DRILL 1/8″ DIA.
1 1/8″ DEEP

1/4″ DIA. DOWEL

DRILL 1/8″ DIA.

1 1/8″

3/8″

1/8″

1 1/2″

SLIDE IN
(DO NOT GLUE)

Dozer Loader: Pins, Shafts, Etc.

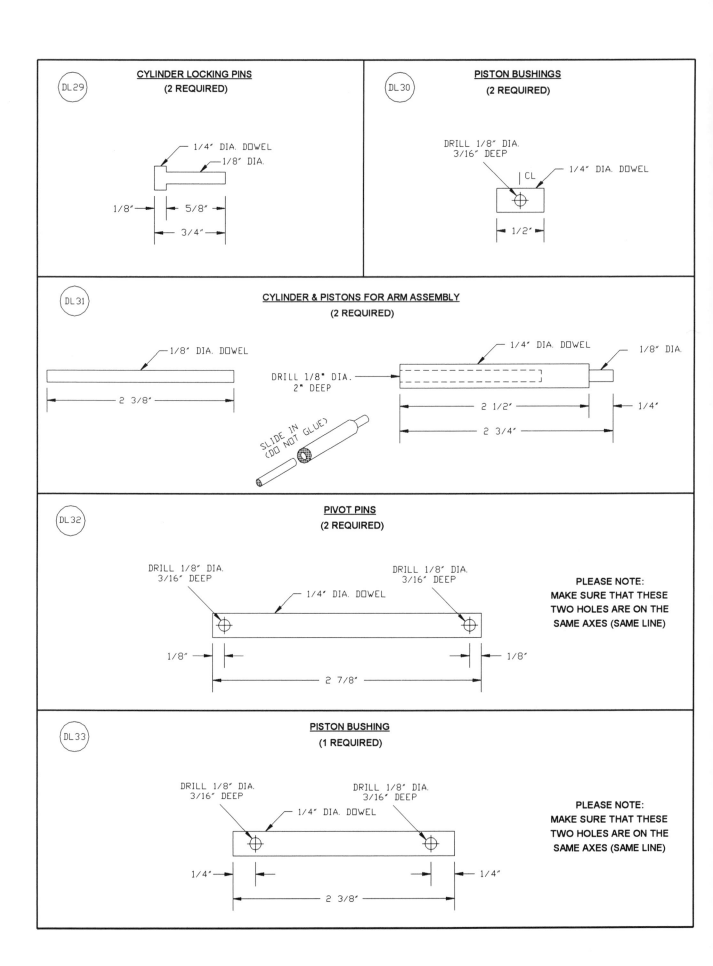

CYLINDER LOCKING PINS
(2 REQUIRED)

DL29

1/4″ DIA. DOWEL
1/8″ DIA.
1/8″
5/8″
3/4″

PISTON BUSHINGS
(2 REQUIRED)

DL30

DRILL 1/8″ DIA.
3/16″ DEEP
CL
1/4″ DIA. DOWEL
1/2″

CYLINDER & PISTONS FOR ARM ASSEMBLY
(2 REQUIRED)

DL31

1/8″ DIA. DOWEL
2 3/8″

DRILL 1/8″ DIA.
2″ DEEP

1/4″ DIA. DOWEL
1/8″ DIA.
2 1/2″
2 3/4″
1/4″

SLIDE IN
(DO NOT GLUE)

PIVOT PINS
(2 REQUIRED)

DL32

DRILL 1/8″ DIA.
3/16″ DEEP
DRILL 1/8″ DIA.
3/16″ DEEP
1/4″ DIA. DOWEL
1/8″
1/8″
2 7/8″

PLEASE NOTE:
MAKE SURE THAT THESE
TWO HOLES ARE ON THE
SAME AXES (SAME LINE)

PISTON BUSHING
(1 REQUIRED)

DL33

DRILL 1/8″ DIA.
3/16″ DEEP
DRILL 1/8″ DIA.
3/16″ DEEP
1/4″ DIA. DOWEL
1/4″
1/4″
2 3/8″

PLEASE NOTE:
MAKE SURE THAT THESE
TWO HOLES ARE ON THE
SAME AXES (SAME LINE)

Dozer Loader: Pins, Shafts, Etc.

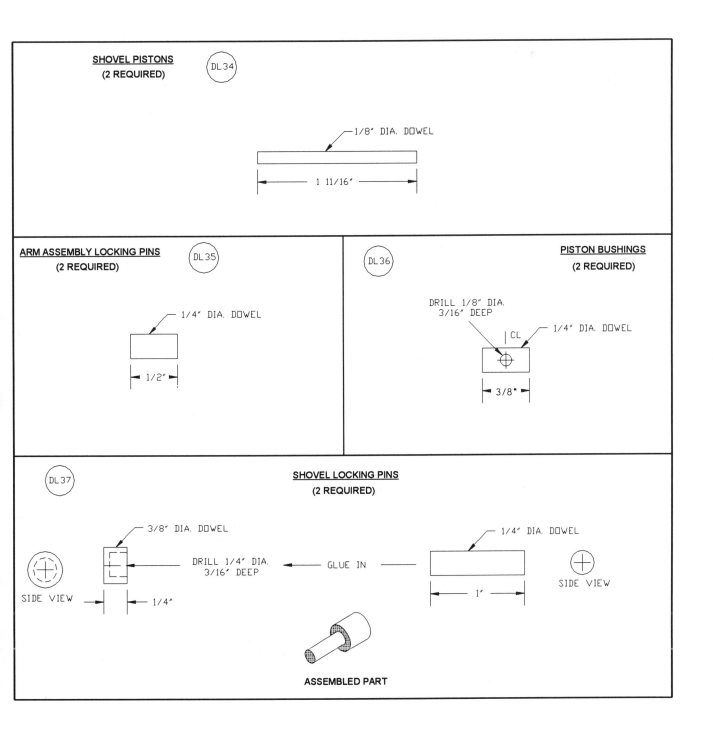

SHOVEL PISTONS
(2 REQUIRED)

DL 34

1/8″ DIA. DOWEL

1 11/16″

ARM ASSEMBLY LOCKING PINS
(2 REQUIRED)

DL 35

1/4″ DIA. DOWEL

1/2″

DL 36

PISTON BUSHINGS
(2 REQUIRED)

DRILL 1/8″ DIA.
3/16″ DEEP

CL

1/4″ DIA. DOWEL

3/8″

DL 37

SHOVEL LOCKING PINS
(2 REQUIRED)

3/8″ DIA. DOWEL

SIDE VIEW

DRILL 1/4″ DIA.
3/16″ DEEP

GLUE IN

1/4″

1/4″ DIA. DOWEL

1″

SIDE VIEW

ASSEMBLED PART

Dozer Loader: Pins, Shafts, Etc.

53

Additional Information - Dozer Loader

Drill holes into body assembly, as shown.

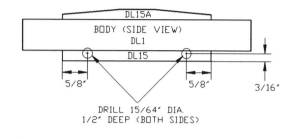

Drill two holes in part DL1A, as shown below.

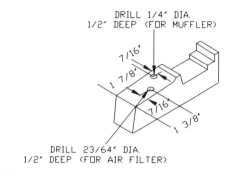

Glue part DL20 onto shovel back, as shown below.

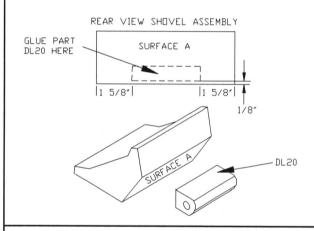

Glue part DL22 onto shovel top, as shown.

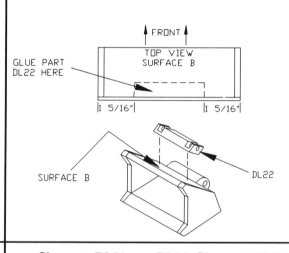

Using your Scroll Saw, cut a groove in part DL24.

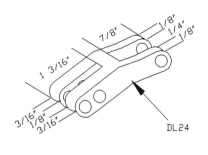

Glue parts DL21 onto DL23. Glue parts DL21 so that they are on the outside of each arm.

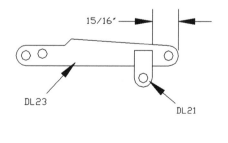

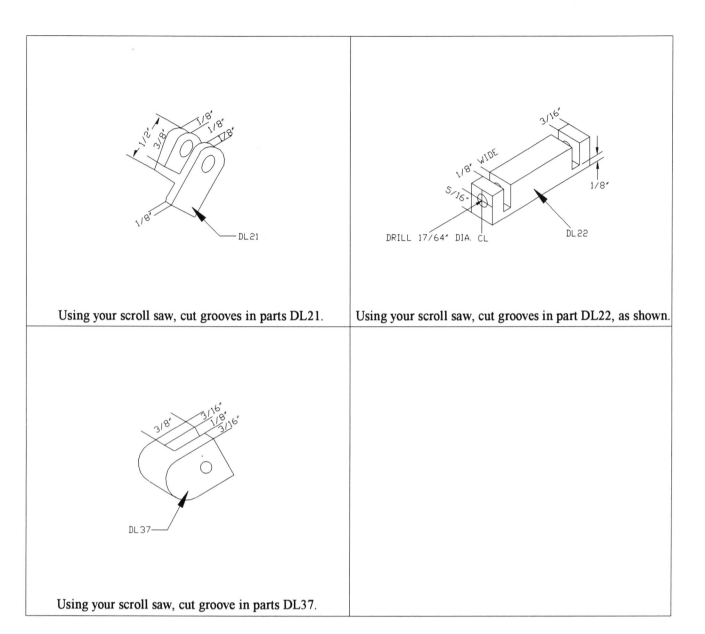

Using your scroll saw, cut grooves in parts DL21.	Using your scroll saw, cut grooves in part DL22, as shown.
Using your scroll saw, cut groove in parts DL37.	

Dozer Loader - Assembly Drawings

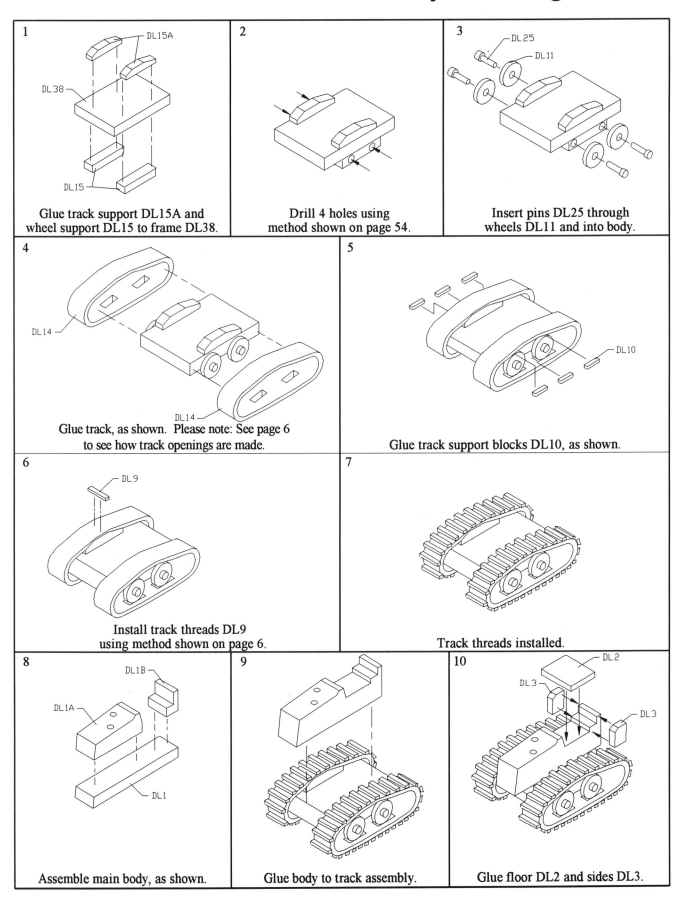

1
Glue track support DL15A and wheel support DL15 to frame DL38.

2
Drill 4 holes using method shown on page 54.

3
Insert pins DL25 through wheels DL11 and into body.

4
Glue track, as shown. Please note: See page 6 to see how track openings are made.

5
Glue track support blocks DL10, as shown.

6
Install track threads DL9 using method shown on page 6.

7
Track threads installed.

8
Assemble main body, as shown.

9
Glue body to track assembly.

10
Glue floor DL2 and sides DL3.

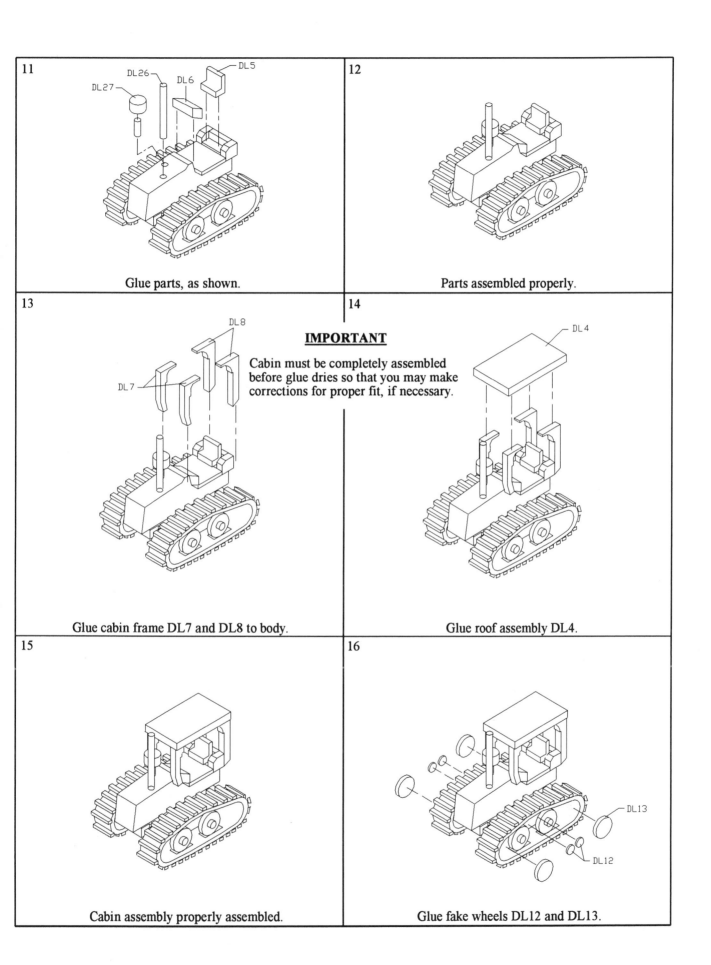

11

DL27 DL26 DL6 DL5

Glue parts, as shown.

12

Parts assembled properly.

13

DL8

DL7

Glue cabin frame DL7 and DL8 to body.

14

<u>IMPORTANT</u>

Cabin must be completely assembled
before glue dries so that you may make
corrections for proper fit, if necessary.

DL4

Glue roof assembly DL4.

15

Cabin assembly properly assembled.

16

DL13

DL12

Glue fake wheels DL12 and DL13.

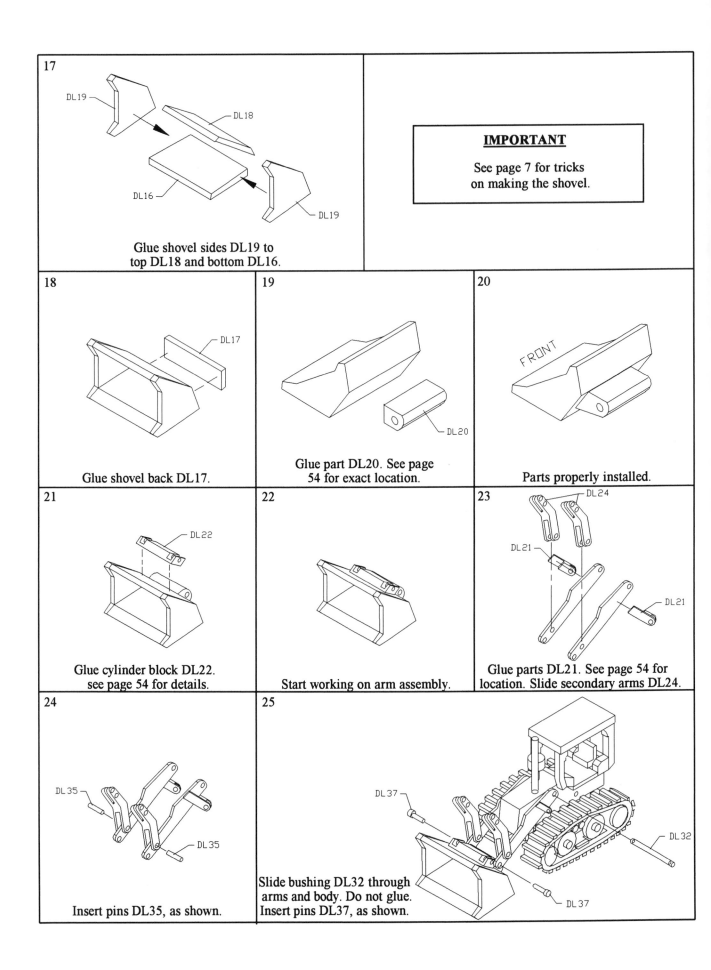

17

DL19

DL18

DL16

DL19

Glue shovel sides DL19 to
top DL18 and bottom DL16.

IMPORTANT

See page 7 for tricks
on making the shovel.

18

DL17

Glue shovel back DL17.

19

DL20

Glue part DL20. See page
54 for exact location.

20

FRONT

Parts properly installed.

21

DL22

Glue cylinder block DL22.
see page 54 for details.

22

Start working on arm assembly.

23

DL24

DL21

DL21

Glue parts DL21. See page 54 for
location. Slide secondary arms DL24.

24

DL35

DL35

Insert pins DL35, as shown.

25

DL37

DL37

DL32

Slide bushing DL32 through
arms and body. Do not glue.
Insert pins DL37, as shown.

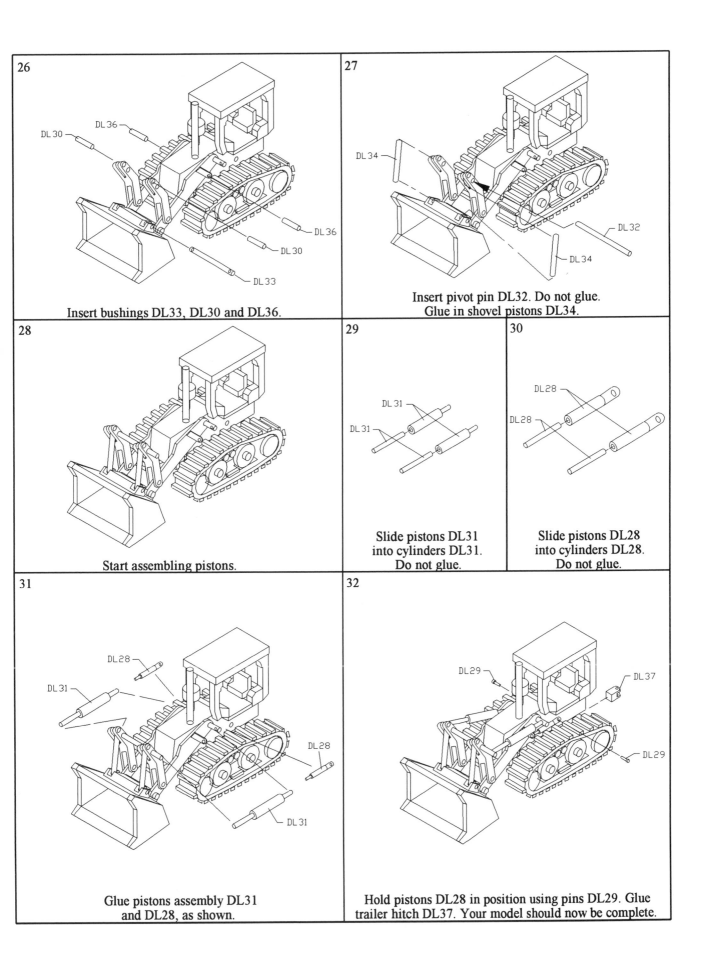

26 Insert bushings DL33, DL30 and DL36.

27 Insert pivot pin DL32. Do not glue.
Glue in shovel pistons DL34.

28 Start assembling pistons.

29 Slide pistons DL31
into cylinders DL31.
Do not glue.

30 Slide pistons DL28
into cylinders DL28.
Do not glue.

31 Glue pistons assembly DL31
and DL28, as shown.

32 Hold pistons DL28 in position using pins DL29. Glue
trailer hitch DL37. Your model should now be complete.

EXCAVATOR

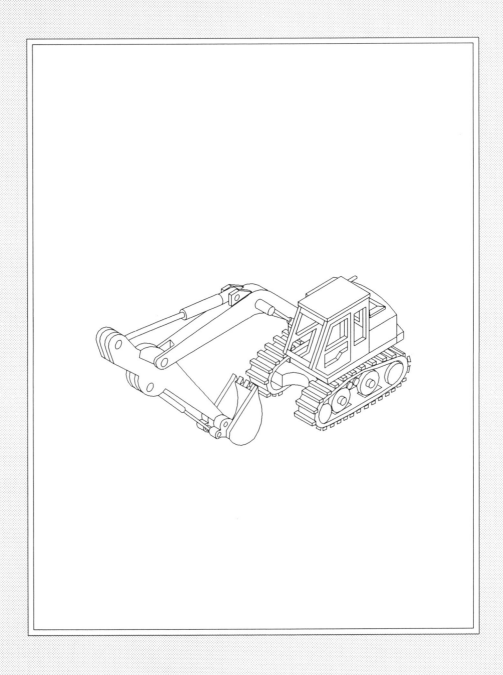

General Instructions - Excavator

1- Start by cutting materials needed by following the list of materials, paying attention to the rough and finished size. **Identify the parts as they are cut.**

Please note: Different types of wood can be used for the various parts. It is suggested, however, that hard wood be used, since many of the parts would be much too fragile if using soft wood. We have used a combination of pine, maple and oak to give the models a nice contrast!

2- Remove the full-size patterns found in the appendix. Cut them out, leaving approximately 1/16" all around, and place on the proper piece of wood. Patterns can be secured to wood using either spray adhesive or rubber ciment. If using the latter, cut and sand the part first to finished size. If drilling is required, mark the hole by inserting a scriber or nail through the pattern into the wood. Remove the pattern before drilling.

You should have no trouble determining which surface to attach most of the patterns. Some parts, however, can be confusing since the pattern could fit on more than one surface. The drawings below indicate exactly which surface to attach the patterns for these parts.

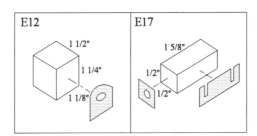

3- Look at the full-size drawing sheets to finish parts E9, E10, and E13.

4- Parts E12, E17, E18 and E28 will need additional cuts and details, please refer to the additional information pages, to complete these parts.

5- Using maple dowels, make all pins, shafts, etc.

6- Follow the assembly drawings to complete your model.

List of Materials - Excavator

Part	T	W	L	Material	Qty.	*
E1	1/4"	3 1/4"	3 1/4"	oak	1	R
E2	1/4"	3 1/4"	3 1/4"	oak	1	R
E3	1/4"	1 7/8"	3 1/4"	oak	1	R
E4	1/4"	2 1/8"	2 7/8"	oak	1	R
E5	1/4"	2 3/16"	2 1/2"	pine	1	F
E6	1/4"	1/4"	1 1/2"	oak	2	F
E7	1/4"	1 3/8" DIA.		maple	4	F
E8	1/4"	3/8"	1"	pine	6	F
E9	3/8"	4 3/8"	5 1/4"	pine	1	F
E10	1/4"	1 1/2"	2 3/4"	pine	1	F
E11	1 1/2"	4 3/8"	3"	pine	1	F
E12	1 1/8"	1 1/4"	1 1/4"	maple	1	R
E13	3/4"	3 1/8"	5 5/8"	pine	1	F
E14	1/4"	2" DIA.		maple	1	F
E15	1/2"	1 3/4" DIA.		maple	1	F

Part	T	W	L	Material	Qty.	*
E16	1/2"	5/8"	1 11/16"	oak	1	F
E17	1/2"	1/2"	1 5/8"	maple	1	F
E18	3/4"	2 7/8"	8 5/8"	maple	1	R
E19	1/4"	5/8"	1 1/2"	maple	2	R
E20	1/8"	1/4"	1 3/8"	pine	72	F
E21	1/4"	1/2"	3 3/4"	pine	2	F
E21A	1/4"	1/2"	3 3/4"	pine	2	R
E22	1/4"	1/2" DIA.		maple	4	F
E23	1/4"	1 1/4" DIA.		maple	4	F
E24	1 1/4"	2"	7"	pine	2	R
E25	1/4"	1 1/2"	5 5/8"	maple	2	R
E26	1/4"	1 5/8"	5 7/8"	maple	1	R
E27	1/4"	1 3/4"	2 1/2"	maple	2	R
E28	1 3/8"	2"	3 1/2"	maple	1	R
E29	3/8"	1 3/8"	4 5/8"	oak	1	R

T = Thickness
W = Width
L = Length

R = Rough size
F = Finished size

Instructions:

R= Rough sizes, the material is cut oversized so you have ample room to apply the pattern on the surface. Sanding is not required at this point.

F = Finished Size: Cut and sand parts to finished size.

Full-Sized Patterns: Set One

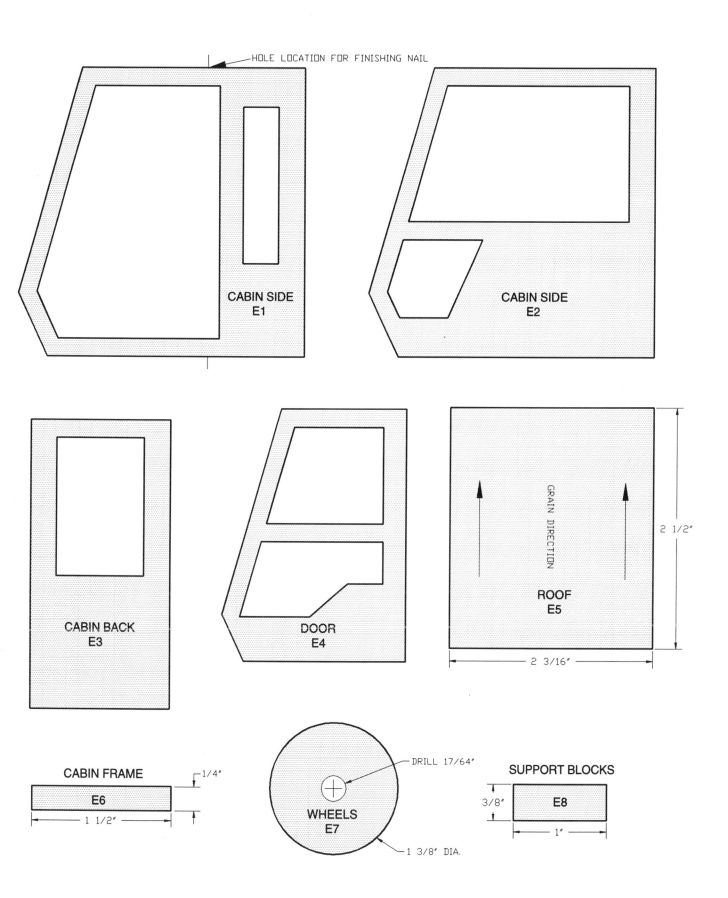

HOLE LOCATION FOR FINISHING NAIL

CABIN SIDE
E1

CABIN SIDE
E2

CABIN BACK
E3

DOOR
E4

GRAIN DIRECTION

ROOF
E5

2 1/2"

2 3/16"

CABIN FRAME

1/4"

E6

1 1/2"

DRILL 17/64"

WHEELS
E7

1 3/8" DIA.

SUPPORT BLOCKS

3/8"

E8

1"

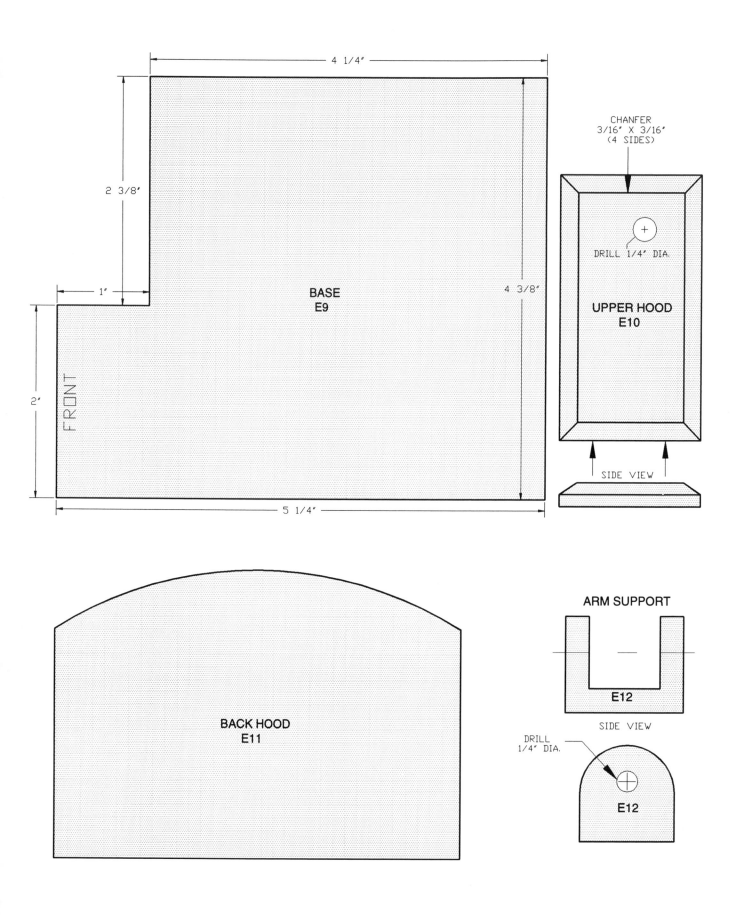

4 1/4"

2 3/8"

1"

FRONT

2"

BASE
E9

4 3/8"

5 1/4"

CHANFER
3/16" X 3/16"
(4 SIDES)

DRILL 1/4" DIA.

UPPER HOOD
E10

SIDE VIEW

ARM SUPPORT

E12

SIDE VIEW

DRILL
1/4" DIA.

E12

BACK HOOD
E11

Excavator: Full-sized Patterns

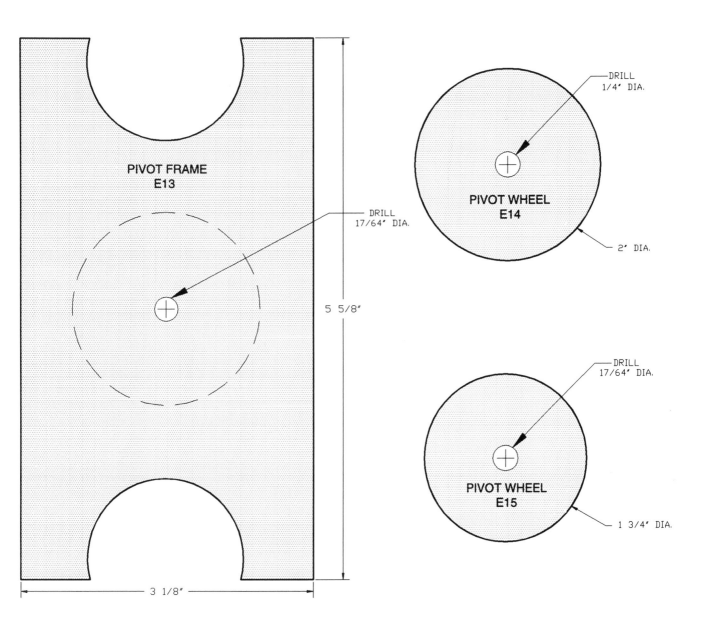

PIVOT FRAME
E13

DRILL
17/64" DIA.

5 5/8"

3 1/8"

PIVOT WHEEL
E14

DRILL
1/4" DIA.

2" DIA.

PIVOT WHEEL
E15

DRILL
17/64" DIA.

1 3/4" DIA.

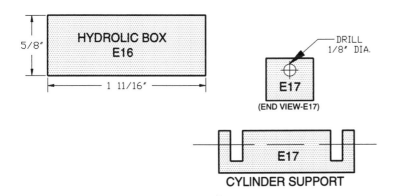

HYDROLIC BOX
E16

5/8"

1 11/16"

DRILL
1/8" DIA.

E17

(END VIEW-E17)

E17

CYLINDER SUPPORT

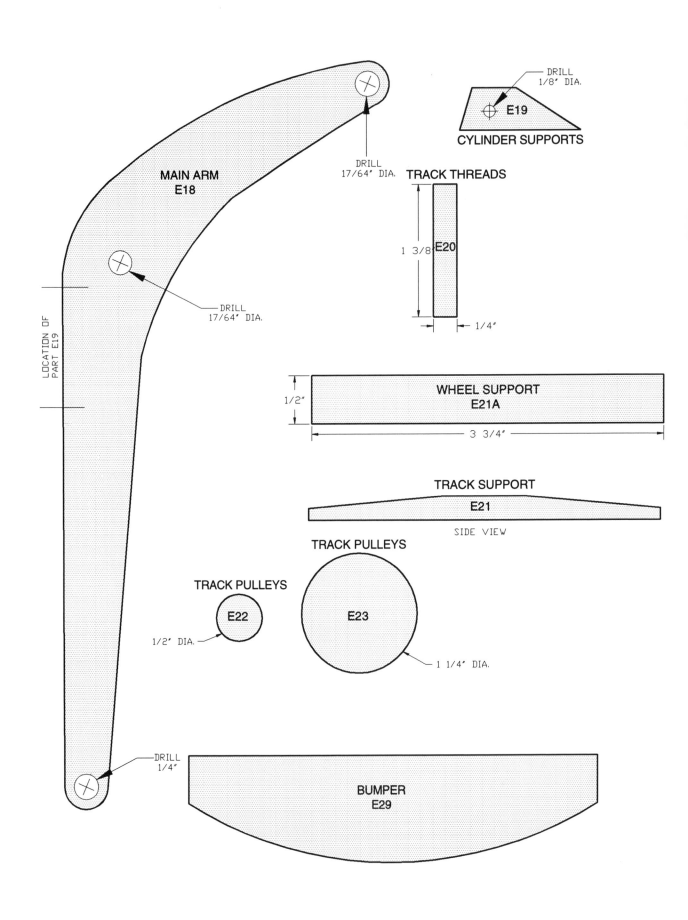

DRILL
1/8" DIA.

E19

CYLINDER SUPPORTS

MAIN ARM
E18

DRILL
17/64" DIA.

TRACK THREADS

E20

1 3/8"

1/4"

DRILL
17/64" DIA.

LOCATION OF
PART E19

WHEEL SUPPORT
E21A

1/2"

3 3/4"

TRACK SUPPORT

E21

SIDE VIEW

TRACK PULLEYS

TRACK PULLEYS

E22

E23

1/2" DIA.

1 1/4" DIA.

DRILL
1/4"

BUMPER
E29

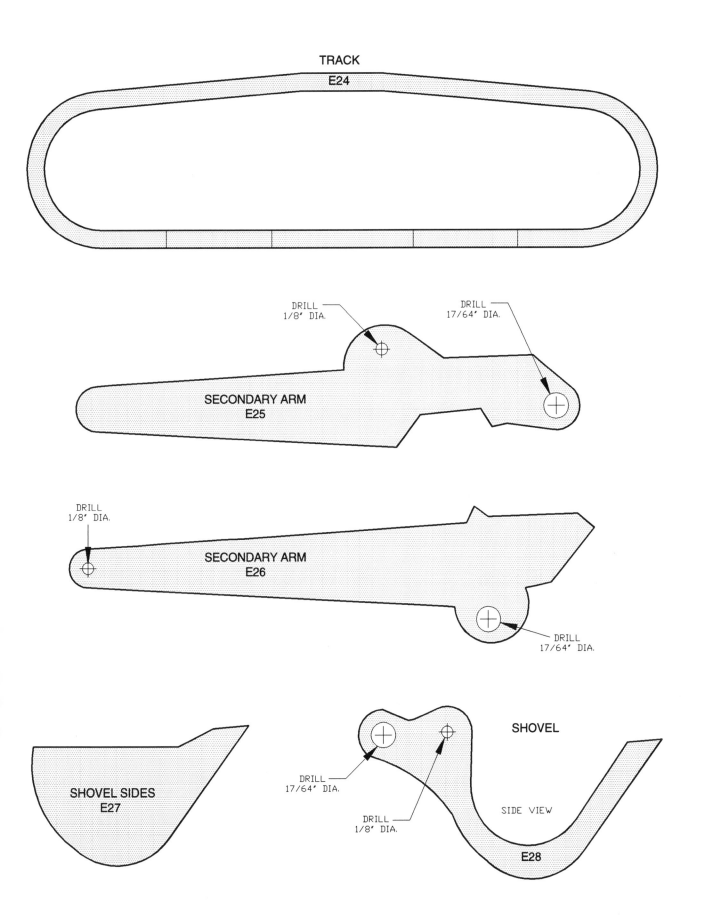

TRACK
E24

DRILL
1/8" DIA.

DRILL
17/64" DIA.

SECONDARY ARM
E25

DRILL
1/8" DIA.

SECONDARY ARM
E26

DRILL
17/64" DIA.

SHOVEL

DRILL
17/64" DIA.

SHOVEL SIDES
E27

DRILL
1/8" DIA.

SIDE VIEW

E28

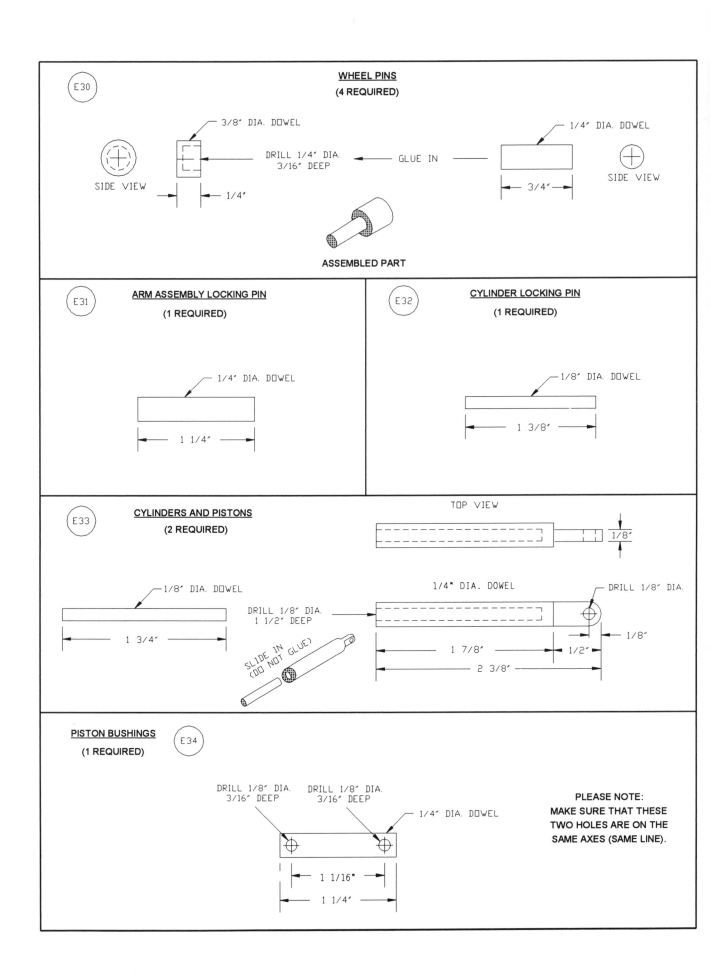

WHEEL PINS
(4 REQUIRED)

E30

3/8" DIA. DOWEL

DRILL 1/4" DIA. 3/16" DEEP

GLUE IN

1/4" DIA. DOWEL

SIDE VIEW

1/4"

3/4"

SIDE VIEW

ASSEMBLED PART

E31

ARM ASSEMBLY LOCKING PIN

(1 REQUIRED)

1/4" DIA. DOWEL

1 1/4"

E32

CYLINDER LOCKING PIN

(1 REQUIRED)

1/8" DIA. DOWEL

1 3/8"

E33

CYLINDERS AND PISTONS

(2 REQUIRED)

TOP VIEW

1/8"

1/8" DIA. DOWEL

1 3/4"

DRILL 1/8" DIA. 1 1/2" DEEP

1/4" DIA. DOWEL

DRILL 1/8" DIA.

1/8"

SLIDE IN (DO NOT GLUE)

1 7/8"

1/2"

2 3/8"

PISTON BUSHINGS

(1 REQUIRED)

E34

DRILL 1/8" DIA. 3/16" DEEP

DRILL 1/8" DIA. 3/16" DEEP

1/4" DIA. DOWEL

PLEASE NOTE:
MAKE SURE THAT THESE
TWO HOLES ARE ON THE
SAME AXES (SAME LINE).

1 1/16"

1 1/4"

Excavator: Pins, Shafts, Etc.

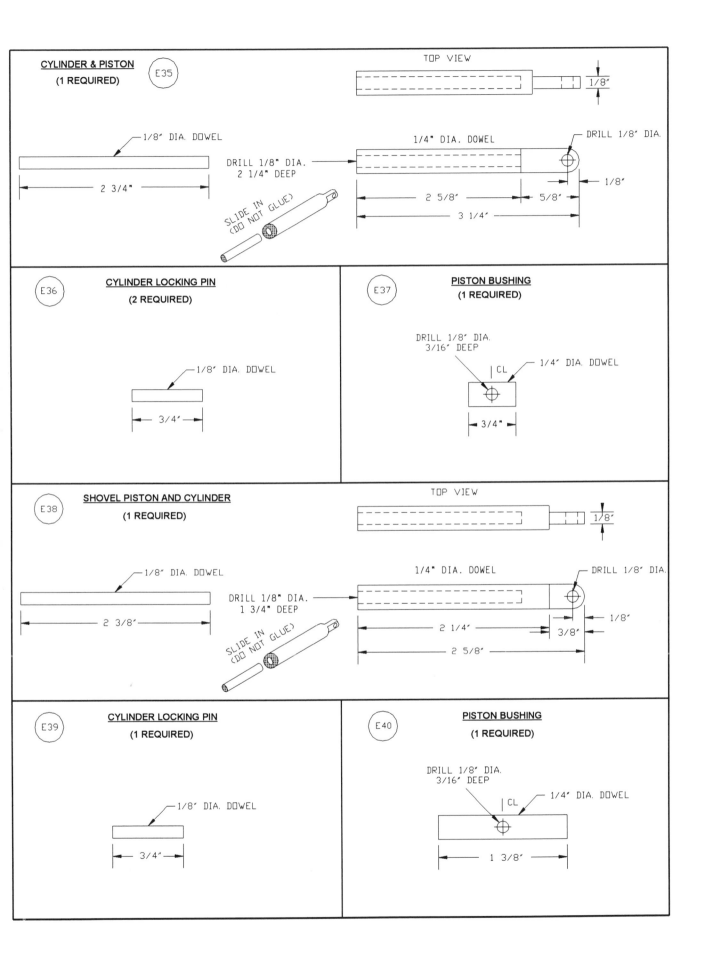

CYLINDER & PISTON
(1 REQUIRED)   E35

TOP VIEW

1/8"

1/8" DIA. DOWEL

DRILL 1/8" DIA.
2 1/4" DEEP

1/4" DIA. DOWEL

DRILL 1/8" DIA.

2 3/4"

SLIDE IN
(DO NOT GLUE)

2 5/8"   5/8"

1/8"

3 1/4"

E36   **CYLINDER LOCKING PIN**
(2 REQUIRED)

1/8" DIA. DOWEL

3/4"

E37   **PISTON BUSHING**
(1 REQUIRED)

DRILL 1/8" DIA.
3/16" DEEP

CL   1/4" DIA. DOWEL

3/4"

E38   **SHOVEL PISTON AND CYLINDER**
(1 REQUIRED)

TOP VIEW

1/8"

1/8" DIA. DOWEL

DRILL 1/8" DIA.
1 3/4" DEEP

1/4" DIA. DOWEL

DRILL 1/8" DIA.

2 3/8"

SLIDE IN
(DO NOT GLUE)

2 1/4"   3/8"

1/8"

2 5/8"

E39   **CYLINDER LOCKING PIN**
(1 REQUIRED)

1/8" DIA. DOWEL

3/4"

E40   **PISTON BUSHING**
(1 REQUIRED)

DRILL 1/8" DIA.
3/16" DEEP

CL   1/4" DIA. DOWEL

1 3/8"

Excavator: Pins, Shafts, Etc.

69

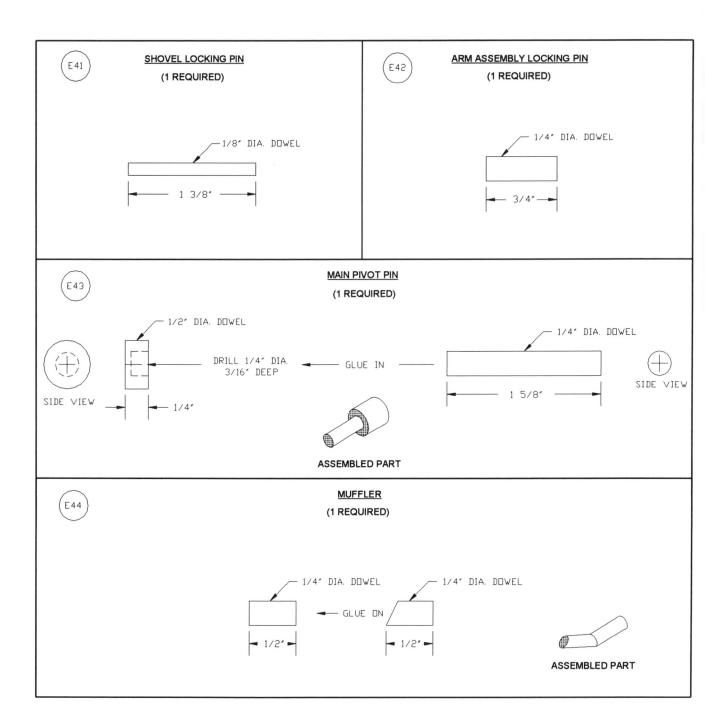

E41 SHOVEL LOCKING PIN
(1 REQUIRED)

1/8″ DIA. DOWEL

1 3/8″

E42 ARM ASSEMBLY LOCKING PIN
(1 REQUIRED)

1/4″ DIA. DOWEL

3/4″

E43 MAIN PIVOT PIN
(1 REQUIRED)

1/2″ DIA. DOWEL

DRILL 1/4″ DIA.
3/16″ DEEP

GLUE IN

1/4″ DIA. DOWEL

1 5/8″

SIDE VIEW

SIDE VIEW

1/4″

ASSEMBLED PART

E44 MUFFLER
(1 REQUIRED)

1/4″ DIA. DOWEL

GLUE ON

1/4″ DIA. DOWEL

1/2″

1/2″

ASSEMBLED PART

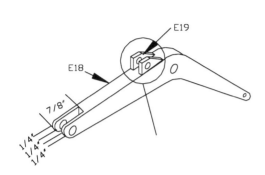

Using your Scroll Saw, cut a groove in part E18.
Glue parts E19. See full-size pattern for details.

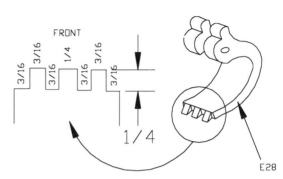

Using your Scroll Saw, cut the grooves in part E28.

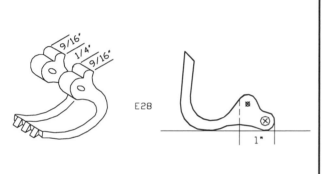

Using your Scroll Saw, cut a groove in part E28.

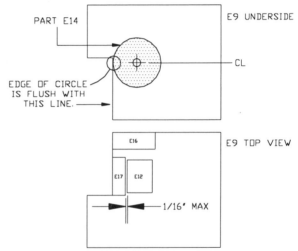

Glue parts E16, E17 and E12 onto base E9.

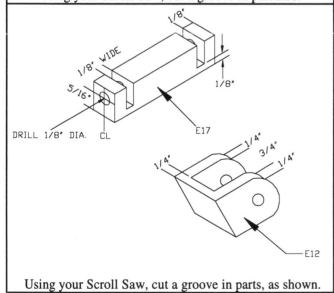

Using your Scroll Saw, cut a groove in parts, as shown.

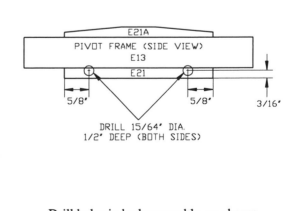

Drill holes in body assembly, as shown.

Excavator - Assembly Drawings

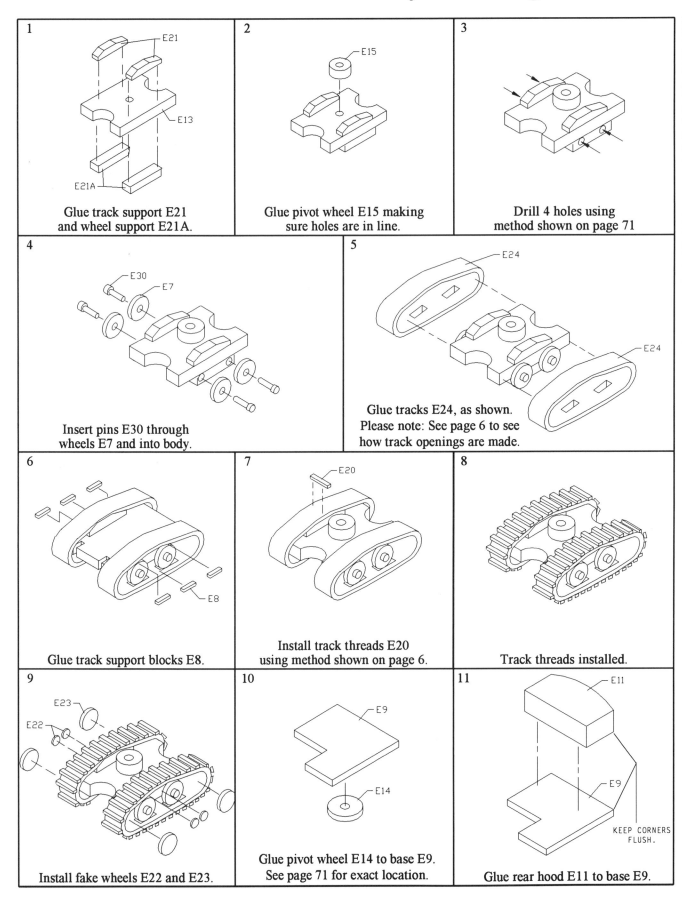

1

Glue track support E21
and wheel support E21A.

2

Glue pivot wheel E15 making
sure holes are in line.

3

Drill 4 holes using
method shown on page 71

4

Insert pins E30 through
wheels E7 and into body.

5

Glue tracks E24, as shown.
Please note: See page 6 to see
how track openings are made.

6

Glue track support blocks E8.

7

Install track threads E20
using method shown on page 6.

8

Track threads installed.

9

Install fake wheels E22 and E23.

10

Glue pivot wheel E14 to base E9.
See page 71 for exact location.

11

KEEP CORNERS
FLUSH.

Glue rear hood E11 to base E9.

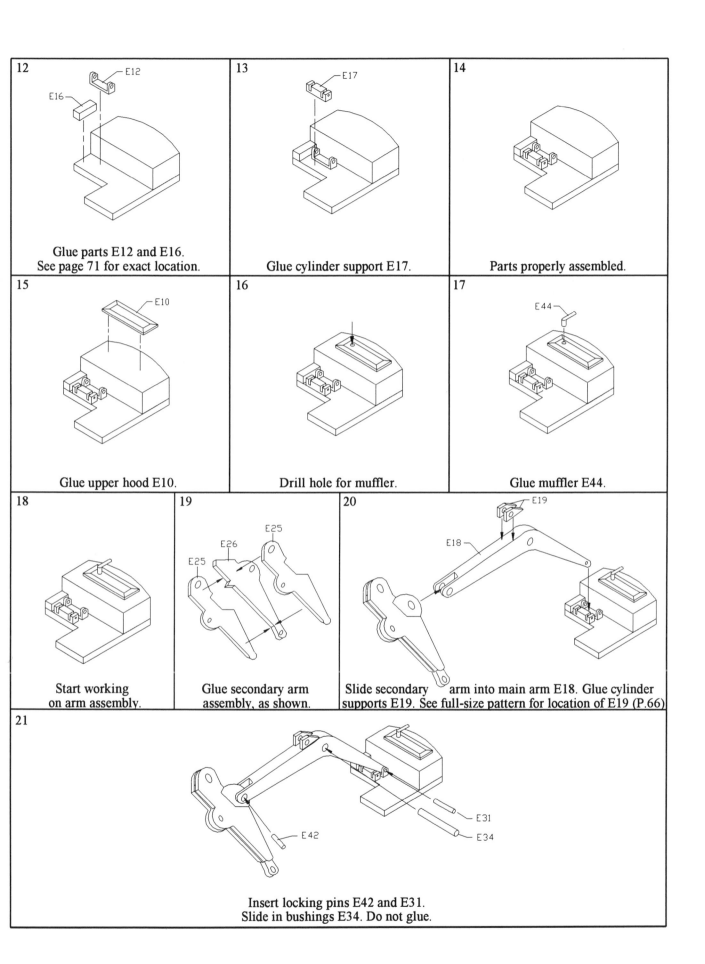

12 Glue parts E12 and E16.
See page 71 for exact location.

13 Glue cylinder support E17.

14 Parts properly assembled.

15 Glue upper hood E10.

16 Drill hole for muffler.

17 Glue muffler E44.

18 Start working
on arm assembly.

19 Glue secondary arm
assembly, as shown.

20 Slide secondary arm into main arm E18. Glue cylinder
supports E19. See full-size pattern for location of E19 (P.66)

21 Insert locking pins E42 and E31.
Slide in bushings E34. Do not glue.

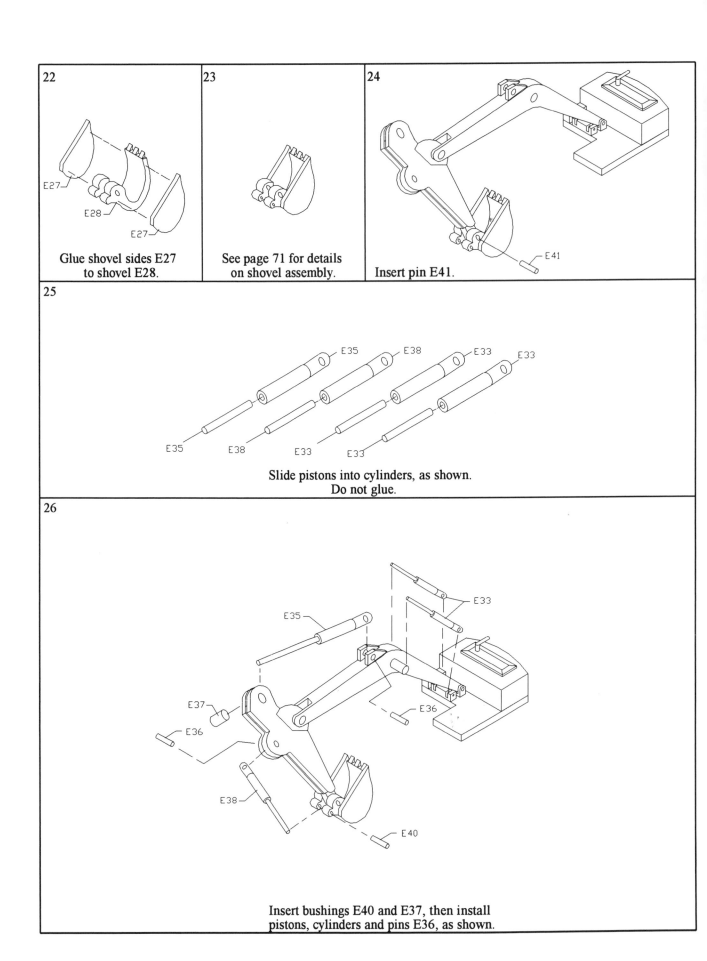

22

Glue shovel sides E27
to shovel E28.

23

See page 71 for details
on shovel assembly.

24

Insert pin E41.

25

Slide pistons into cylinders, as shown.
Do not glue.

26

Insert bushings E40 and E37, then install
pistons, cylinders and pins E36, as shown.

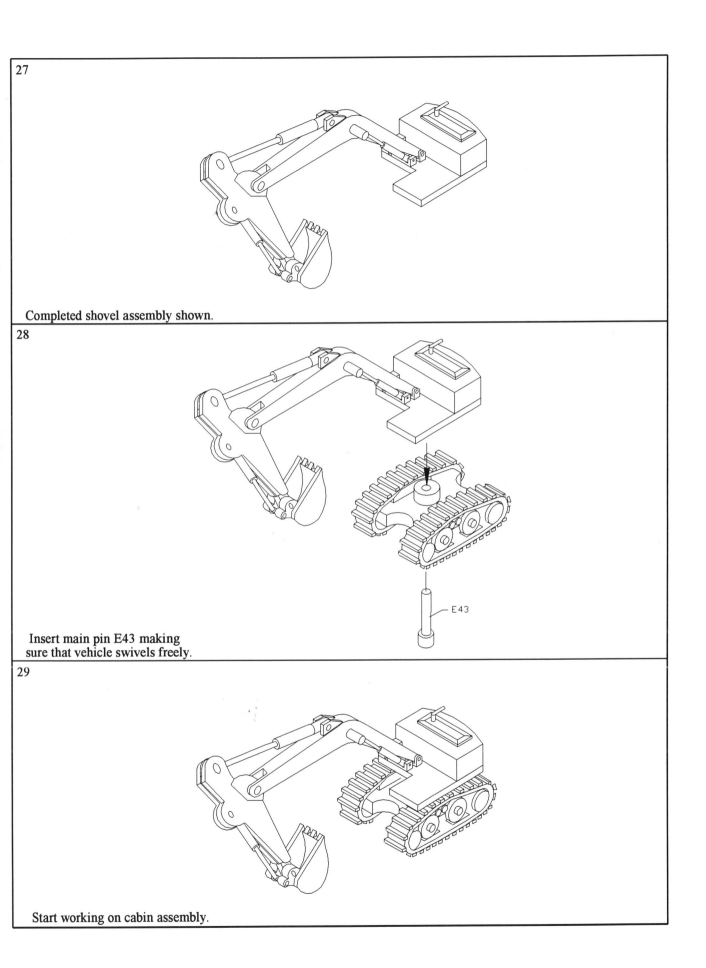

27

Completed shovel assembly shown.

28

E43

Insert main pin E43 making
sure that vehicle swivels freely.

29

Start working on cabin assembly.

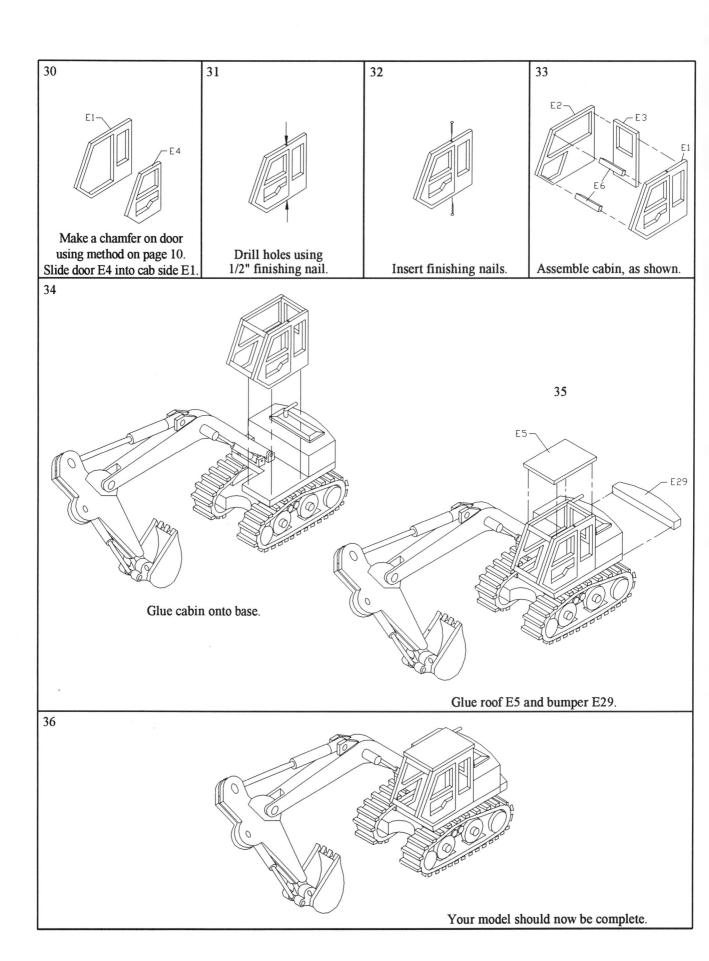

30

Make a chamfer on door using method on page 10. Slide door E4 into cab side E1.

31

Drill holes using 1/2" finishing nail.

32

Insert finishing nails.

33

Assemble cabin, as shown.

34

Glue cabin onto base.

35

Glue roof E5 and bumper E29.

36

Your model should now be complete.

GRADER

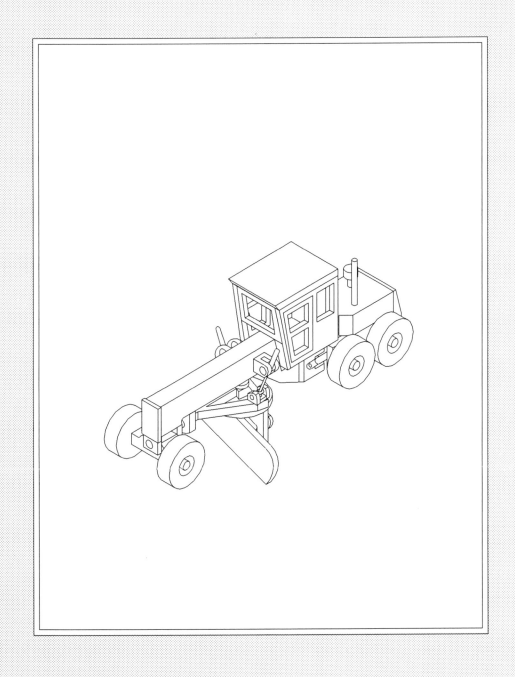

General Instructions - Grader

1- Start by cutting materials needed by following the list of materials, paying attention to the rough and finished size. **Identify the parts as they are cut.**

Please note: Different types of wood can be used for the various parts. It is suggested, however, that hard wood be used, since many of the parts would be much too fragile if using soft wood. We have used a combination of pine, maple and oak to give the models a nice contrast!

2- Remove the full-size patterns found in the appendix. Cut them out, leaving approximately 1/16" all around, and place on the proper piece of wood. Patterns can be secured to wood using either spray adhesive or rubber ciment. If using the latter, cut and sand the part first to finished size. If drilling is required, mark the hole by inserting a scriber or nail through the pattern into the wood. Remove the pattern before drilling.

You should have no trouble determining which surface to attach most of the patterns. Some parts, however, can be confusing since the pattern could fit on more than one surface. The drawings below indicate exactly which surface to attach the patterns for these parts.

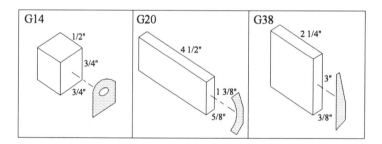

3- Look at the full-size drawing sheets to finish parts G2, G13, G17, G19 and G40.

4- Parts G7, G9, G14, G15 and G21 will need additional cuts and details, please refer to the additional information pages, to complete these parts.

5- Using maple dowels, make all pins, shafts, etc.

6- Follow the assembly drawings to complete your model.

List of Materials - Grader

Part	T	W	L	Material	Qty.	*
G1	1/4"	3"	3 1/4"	oak	2	R
G2	1/4"	2 3/8"	3 1/8"	pine	1	F
G3	1/4"	2"	3 1/4"	oak	1	R
G4	1/4"	2"	2 1/2"	oak	1	R
G5	1/4"	1 7/8"	2 7/8"	oak	2	R
G6	1/4"	2 1/4"	2 1/4"	pine	1	F
G7	1/2"	1"	2 1/2"	maple	1	R
G7A	3/8"	7/8" DIA.		maple	1	F
G8	3/8"	1 1/4"	1 3/8"	maple	1	R
G9	3/8"	2 1/2"	4 1/8"	maple	1	R
G10	1/4"	1 1/8"	2 1/2"	maple	1	R
G11	5/16"	1/2"	1"	maple	1	R
G12	1/8"	5/8"	1 1/4"	maple	1	R

Part	T	W	L	Material	Qty.	*
G13	1 1/2"	2 1/4"	3 7/8"	pine	1	F
G14	1/2"	3/4"	3/4"	maple	2	R
G15	3/4"	1 1/8"	1 3/8"	maple	2	R
G16	3/8"	1 3/8"	4 5/8"	pine	2	F
G17	1/2"	1 1/2"	3 7/8"	pine	2	F
G18	3/8"	3/4"	3 7/8"	pine	1	F
G19	1"	2 1/2" DIA.		oak	6	F
G20	5/8"	1 3/8"	4 1/2"	pine	1	R
G21	1"	3 1/8"	10 1/8"	pine	1	R
G38	3/8"	2 1/4"	3"	pine	1	F
G39	7/8"	1"	1"	maple	1	R
G40	1/4"	2 1/4" DIA.		maple	1	F

R = Rough size
F = Finished size

T = Thickness
W = Width
L = Length

Instructions:

R= Rough sizes, the material is cut oversized so you have ample room to apply the pattern on the surface. Sanding is not required at this point.

F = Finished Size: Cut and sand parts to finished size.

Full-Sized Patterns: Set One

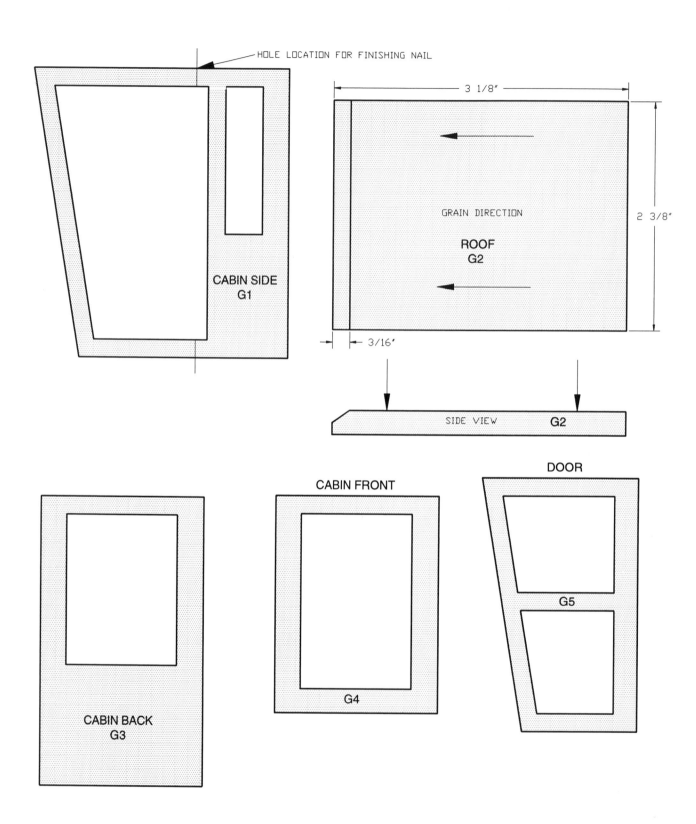

HOLE LOCATION FOR FINISHING NAIL

CABIN SIDE
G1

3 1/8″

GRAIN DIRECTION

ROOF
G2

2 3/8″

3/16″

SIDE VIEW   G2

DOOR

CABIN FRONT

G5

CABIN BACK
G3

G4

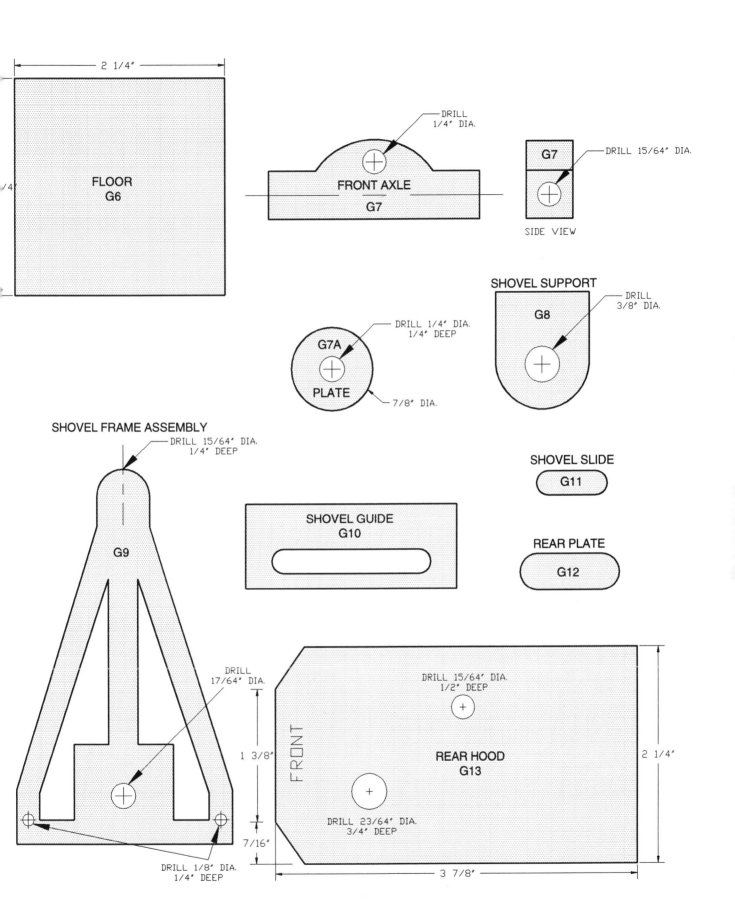

FLOOR
G6

2 1/4"

DRILL
1/4" DIA.

FRONT AXLE
G7

G7

DRILL 15/64" DIA.

SIDE VIEW

DRILL 1/4" DIA.
1/4" DEEP

G7A

PLATE

7/8" DIA.

SHOVEL SUPPORT

G8

DRILL
3/8" DIA.

SHOVEL FRAME ASSEMBLY

DRILL 15/64" DIA.
1/4" DEEP

G9

SHOVEL GUIDE
G10

SHOVEL SLIDE

G11

REAR PLATE

G12

DRILL
17/64" DIA.

DRILL
15/64" DIA.
1/2" DEEP

FRONT

REAR HOOD
G13

1 3/8"

2 1/4"

DRILL 23/64" DIA.
3/4" DEEP

7/16"

DRILL 1/8" DIA.
1/4" DEEP

3 7/8"

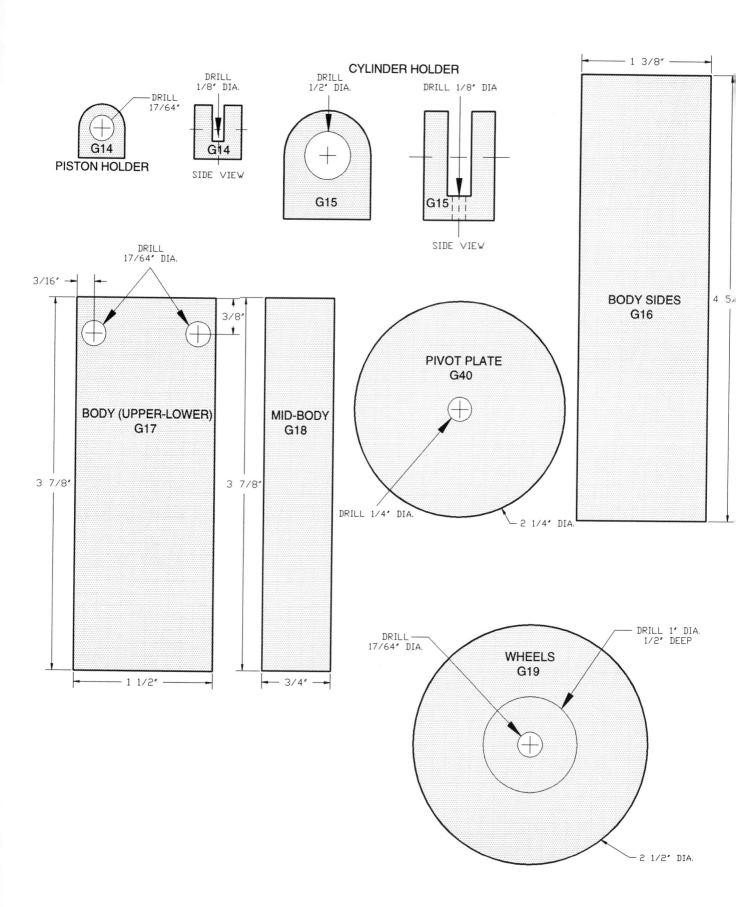

CYLINDER HOLDER

DRILL 17/64"

G14

PISTON HOLDER

DRILL 1/8" DIA.

G14

SIDE VIEW

DRILL 1/2" DIA.

G15

DRILL 1/8" DIA

G15

SIDE VIEW

1 3/8"

BODY SIDES
G16

4 5/

DRILL 17/64" DIA.

3/16"

3/8"

BODY (UPPER-LOWER)
G17

3 7/8"

MID-BODY
G18

3 7/8"

1 1/2"

3/4"

PIVOT PLATE
G40

DRILL 1/4" DIA.

2 1/4" DIA.

DRILL 17/64" DIA.

DRILL 1" DIA. 1/2" DEEP

WHEELS
G19

2 1/2" DIA.

Grader: Full-sized Patterns

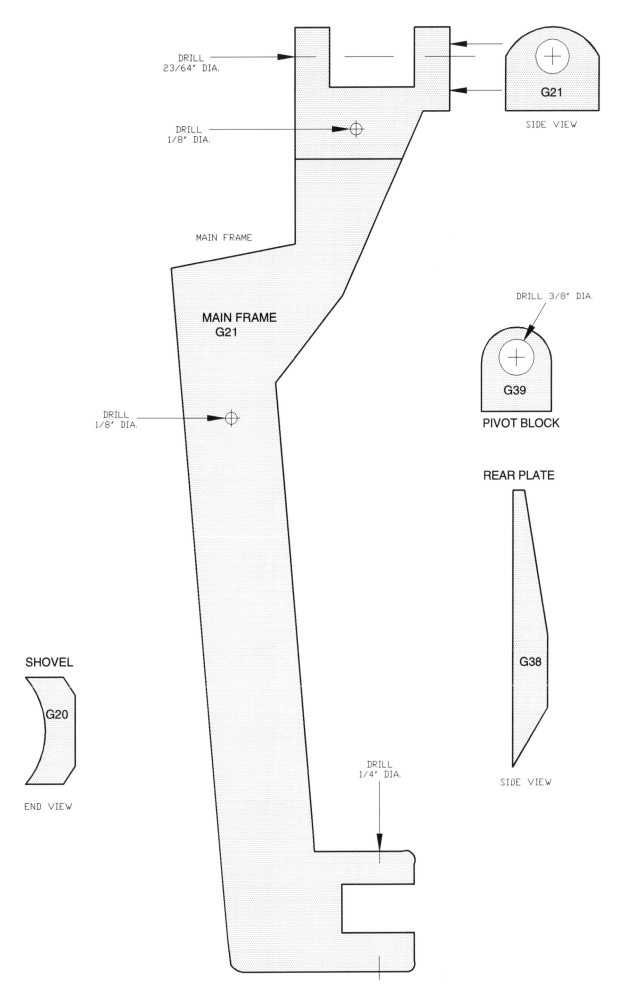

DRILL
23/64″ DIA.

DRILL
1/8″ DIA.

G21

SIDE VIEW

MAIN FRAME

MAIN FRAME
G21

DRILL 3/8″ DIA.

G39

PIVOT BLOCK

DRILL
1/8″ DIA.

REAR PLATE

G38

DRILL
1/4″ DIA.

SIDE VIEW

SHOVEL

G20

END VIEW

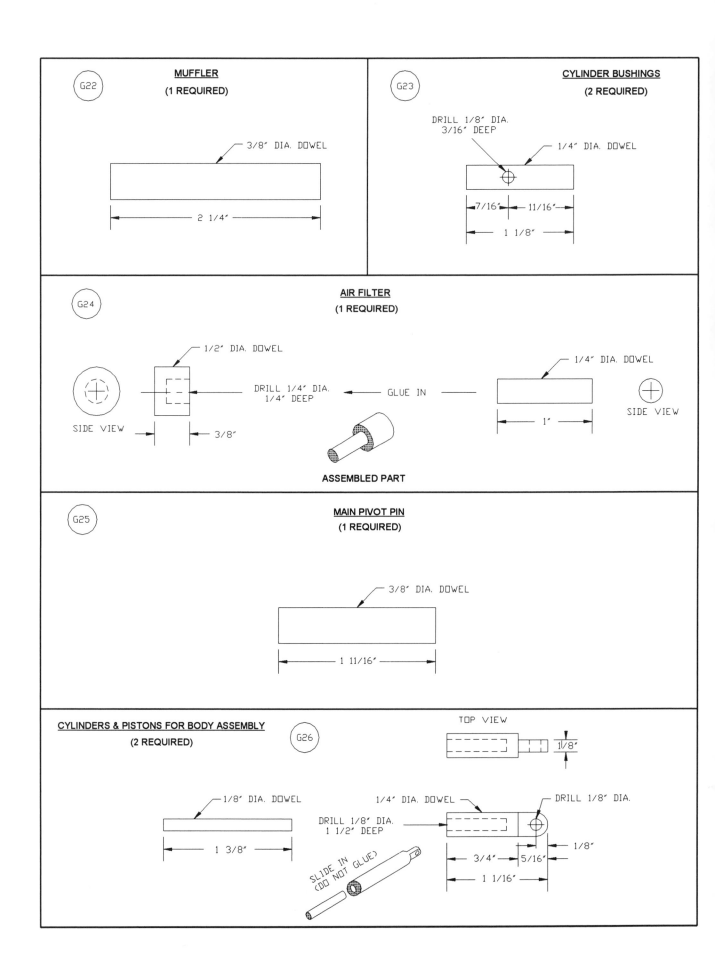

MUFFLER
(1 REQUIRED)

G22

3/8″ DIA. DOWEL

2 1/4″

CYLINDER BUSHINGS
(2 REQUIRED)

G23

DRILL 1/8″ DIA.
3/16″ DEEP

1/4″ DIA. DOWEL

7/16″   11/16″

1 1/8″

AIR FILTER
(1 REQUIRED)

G24

1/2″ DIA. DOWEL

SIDE VIEW

3/8″

DRILL 1/4″ DIA.
1/4″ DEEP

GLUE IN

1/4″ DIA. DOWEL

1″

SIDE VIEW

ASSEMBLED PART

MAIN PIVOT PIN
(1 REQUIRED)

G25

3/8″ DIA. DOWEL

1 11/16″

CYLINDERS & PISTONS FOR BODY ASSEMBLY
(2 REQUIRED)

G26

TOP VIEW

1/8″

1/8″ DIA. DOWEL

1 3/8″

1/4″ DIA. DOWEL

DRILL 1/8″ DIA.
1 1/2″ DEEP

SLIDE IN
(DO NOT GLUE)

DRILL 1/8″ DIA.

1/8″

3/4″   5/16″

1 1/16″

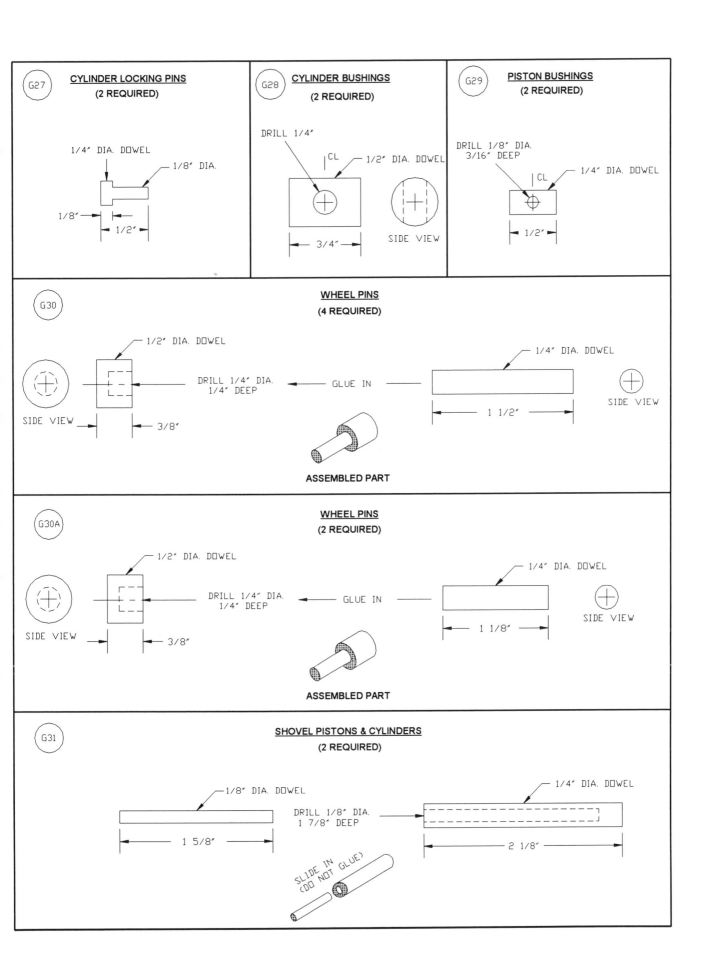

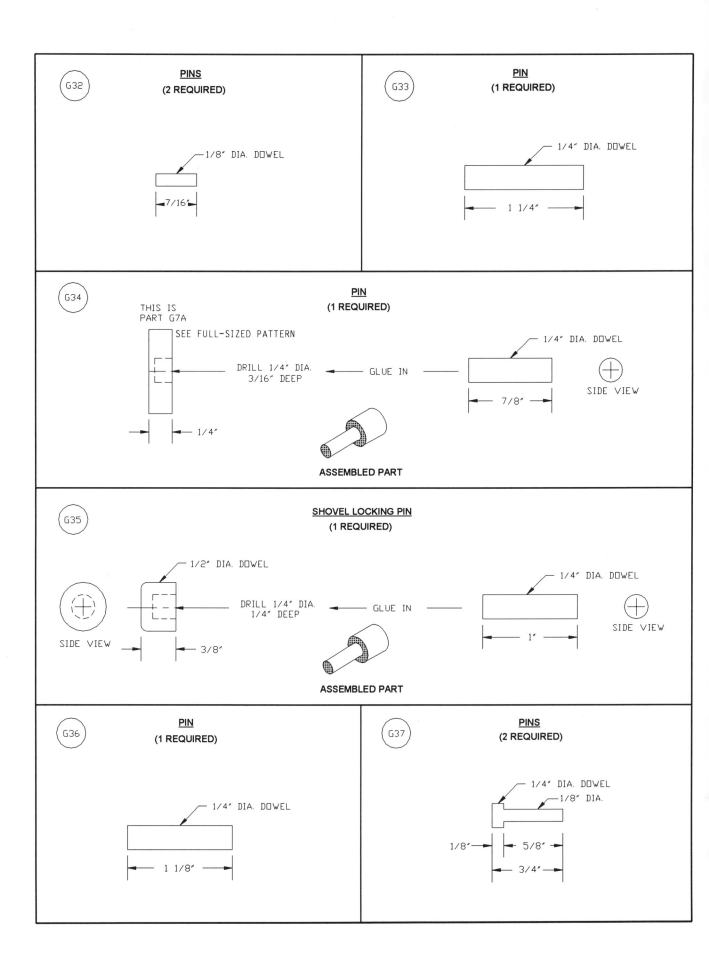

G32

PINS
(2 REQUIRED)

1/8" DIA. DOWEL

7/16"

G33

PIN
(1 REQUIRED)

1/4" DIA. DOWEL

1 1/4"

G34

PIN
(1 REQUIRED)

THIS IS
PART G7A

SEE FULL-SIZED PATTERN

DRILL 1/4" DIA.
3/16" DEEP ← GLUE IN ← 1/4" DIA. DOWEL

7/8"

1/4"

SIDE VIEW

ASSEMBLED PART

G35

SHOVEL LOCKING PIN
(1 REQUIRED)

1/2" DIA. DOWEL

DRILL 1/4" DIA.
1/4" DEEP ← GLUE IN ← 1/4" DIA. DOWEL

1"

SIDE VIEW

3/8"

SIDE VIEW

ASSEMBLED PART

G36

PIN
(1 REQUIRED)

1/4" DIA. DOWEL

1 1/8"

G37

PINS
(2 REQUIRED)

1/4" DIA. DOWEL

1/8" DIA.

1/8"

5/8"

3/4"

G21

PART G8

1/2" SPACE

Glue part G8 onto Main frame G21.

DRILL 1/4" DIA.

THIS VIEW SHOWN FROM ABOVE.

1 3/8"
SAND TO 3/4" WIDE.

1 1/2"

1"

CL

3/8"

DRILL 23/64" DIA.

5/16"

CL

Sand frame G21 to 3/4" wide and drill hole, as shown.

7/8" 1/4" 1/4"

DRILL 9/64"

CL

CL

G15

3/8" 3/16" 1/8" 3/16"

CL

DRILL 1/8" DIA.

CL

G14

Cut grooves and drill holes, as shown.

G9

CL

CL

DRILL 15/64" DIA.
1/4" DEEP

Drill hole in part G9, as shown.

G7

CL

DRILL 15/64" DIA.
3/4" DEEP
(BOTH SIDES)

CL

Drill holes in part G7, as shown.

1/4"

1/2" 3 1/8"

DRILL 15/64" DIA.
(FROM SIDE TO SIDE)

Drill holes in body sides G16.

DRILL 15/64" DIA.
1/2" DEEP

DRILL 23/64" DIA.
3/4" DEEP

5/8"

2"

3/4"

1"

Drill holes in rear hood G13.

G23

11/16"

7/16"

SHORT END DOWN.

Insert bushings G23, as shown.
Do not glue. Short end goes in first.

Grader - Assembly Drawings

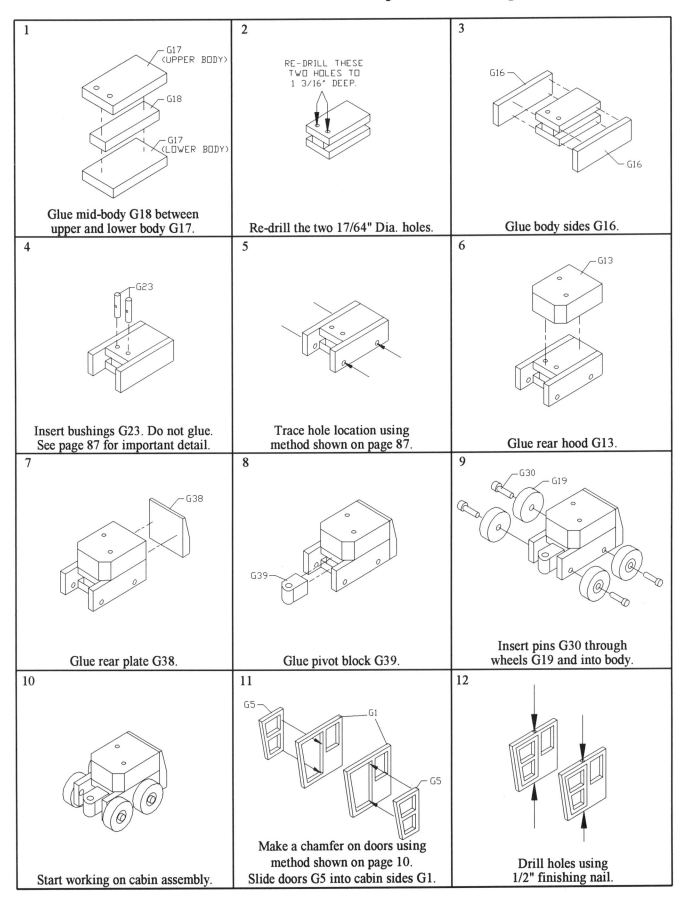

1 Glue mid-body G18 between upper and lower body G17.

2 Re-drill the two 17/64" Dia. holes.

RE-DRILL THESE TWO HOLES TO 1 3/16" DEEP.

3 Glue body sides G16.

4 Insert bushings G23. Do not glue. See page 87 for important detail.

5 Trace hole location using method shown on page 87.

6 Glue rear hood G13.

7 Glue rear plate G38.

8 Glue pivot block G39.

9 Insert pins G30 through wheels G19 and into body.

10 Start working on cabin assembly.

11 Make a chamfer on doors using method shown on page 10. Slide doors G5 into cabin sides G1.

12 Drill holes using 1/2" finishing nail.

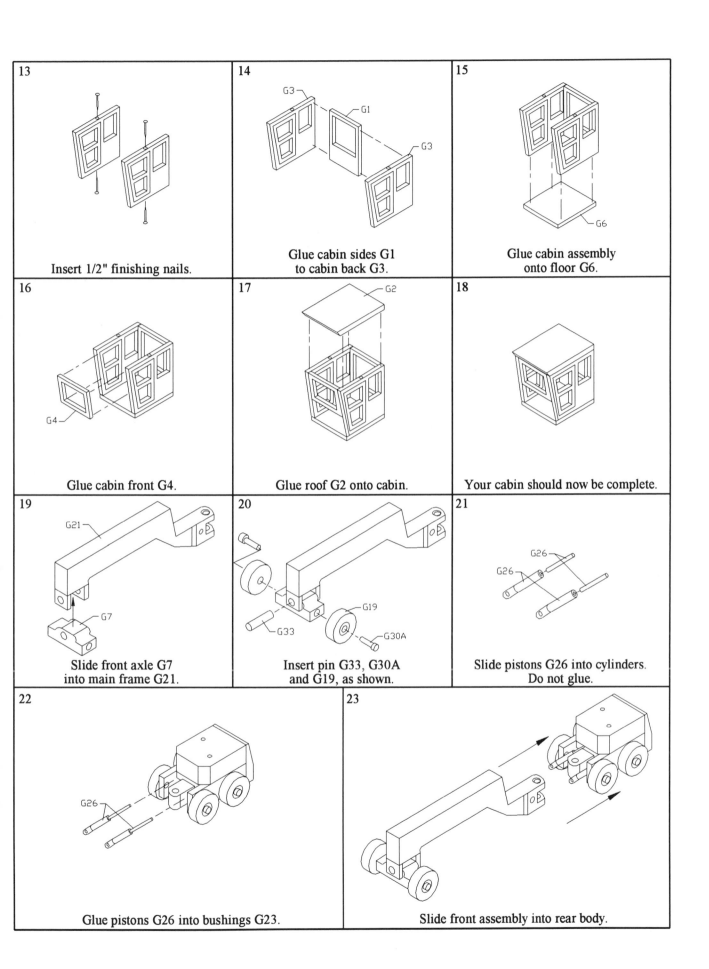

13

Insert 1/2" finishing nails.

14

Glue cabin sides G1
to cabin back G3.

15

Glue cabin assembly
onto floor G6.

16

Glue cabin front G4.

17

Glue roof G2 onto cabin.

18

Your cabin should now be complete.

19

Slide front axle G7
into main frame G21.

20

Insert pin G33, G30A
and G19, as shown.

21

Slide pistons G26 into cylinders.
Do not glue.

22

Glue pistons G26 into bushings G23.

23

Slide front assembly into rear body.

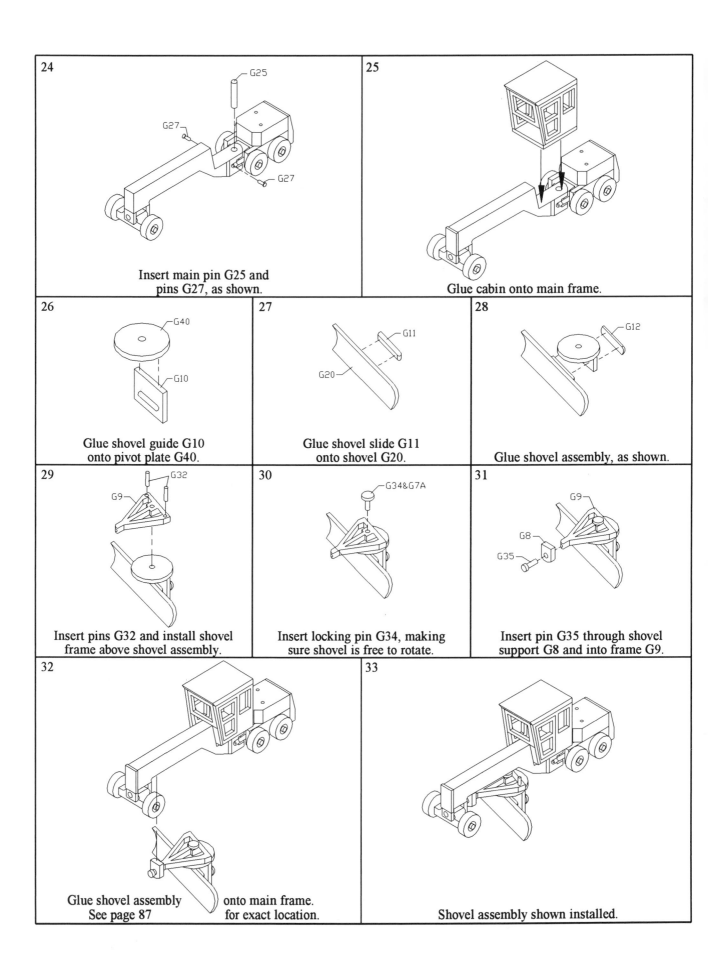

24

Insert main pin G25 and
pins G27, as shown.

25

Glue cabin onto main frame.

26

Glue shovel guide G10
onto pivot plate G40.

27

Glue shovel slide G11
onto shovel G20.

28

Glue shovel assembly, as shown.

29

Insert pins G32 and install shovel
frame above shovel assembly.

30

Insert locking pin G34, making
sure shovel is free to rotate.

31

Insert pin G35 through shovel
support G8 and into frame G9.

32

Glue shovel assembly   onto main frame.
See page 87   for exact location.

33

Shovel assembly shown installed.

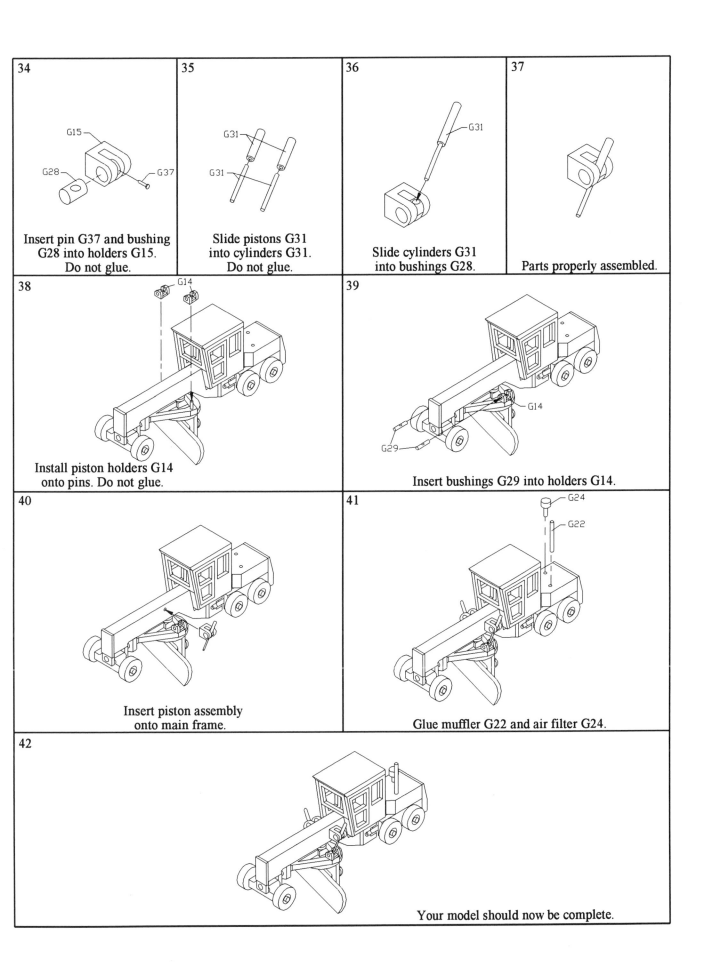

34

Insert pin G37 and bushing
G28 into holders G15.
Do not glue.

35

Slide pistons G31
into cylinders G31.
Do not glue.

36

Slide cylinders G31
into bushings G28.

37

Parts properly assembled.

38

Install piston holders G14
onto pins. Do not glue.

39

Insert bushings G29 into holders G14.

40

Insert piston assembly
onto main frame.

41

Glue muffler G22 and air filter G24.

42

Your model should now be complete.

SKIDDER

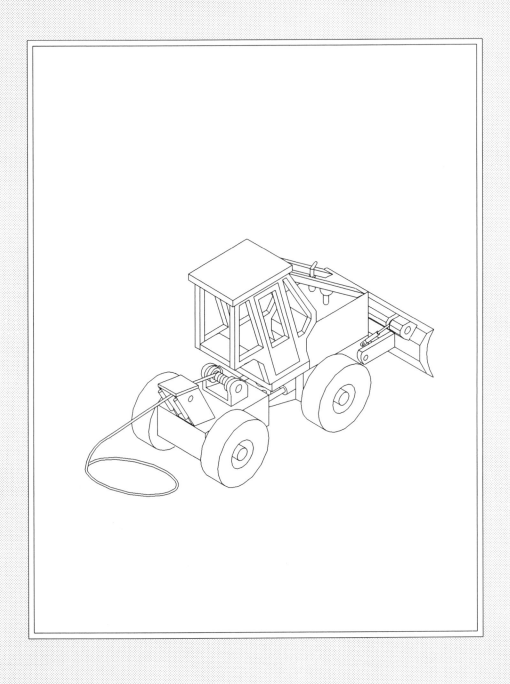

General Instructions - Skidder

1- Start by cutting materials needed by following the list of materials, paying attention to the rough and finished size. **Identify the parts as they are cut.**

Please note: Different types of wood can be used for the various parts. It is suggested, however, that hard wood be used, since many of the parts would be much too fragile if using soft wood. We have used a combination of pine, maple and oak to give the models a nice contrast!

2- Remove the full-size patterns found in the appendix. Cut them out, leaving approximately 1/16" all around, and place on the proper piece of wood. Patterns can be secured to wood using either spray adhesive or rubber ciment. If using the latter, cut and sand the part first to finished size. If drilling is required, mark the hole by inserting a scriber or nail through the pattern into the wood. Remove the pattern before drilling.

You should have no trouble determining which surface to attach most of the patterns. Some parts, however, can be confusing since the pattern could fit on more than one surface. The drawings below indicate exactly which surface to attach the patterns for these parts.

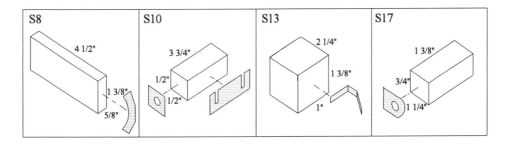

3- Look at the full-size drawing sheets to finish parts S2, S6 and S16.

4- Parts S10, S15 and S17 will need additional cuts and details, please refer to the additional information pages, to complete these parts.

5- Using maple dowels, make all pins, shafts, etc.

6- Follow the assembly drawings to complete your model.

List of Materials - Skidder

Part	T	W	L	Material	Qty.	*
S1	3/8"	2 1/2"	5 1/2"	pine	2	R
S2	1/2"	2 1/4"	4 1/2"	pine	1	F
S3	1/4"	1 1/4"	4 1/4"	pine	2	F
S4	1/4"	2 3/4"	2"	pine	1	F
S5	1 1/4"	2 3/4"	3"	pine	1	F
S6	1 1/2"	2 3/4"	3 1/8"	pine	1	F
S7	1/4"	3"	2 1/2"	pine	1	F
S8	5/8"	1 3/8"	4 1/2"	pine	1	F
S9	1/4"	3/4"	2 1/4"	maple	2	F
S10	1/2"	1/2"	3 3/4"	maple	1	F
S11	1/4"	3 1/4"	3 1/4"	oak	2	R

Part	T	W	L	Material	Qty.	*
S12	1/4"	1 3/8"	2 3/4"	oak	2	R
S13	1"	1 3/8"	2 1/4"	pine	1	R
S14	1/4"	3/8"	3 3/4"	oak	2	R
S15	1/2"	1 1/8"	2 1/4"	maple	1	R
S16	1 1/4"	3" DIA.		oak	4	F
S17	3/4"	1 1/4"	1 3/8"	maple	1	F
S18	1/8"	1"	1 1/8"	maple	1	F
S19	1/8"	1/2" DIA.		maple	2	F
S20	1/8"	3/4" DIA.		maple	2	F
S35	1"	1 1/4"	2 7/8"	maple	1	R

R = Rough size
F = Finished size

T = Thickness
W = Width
L = Length

Instructions:

R= Rough sizes, the material is cut oversized so you have ample room to apply the pattern on the surface. Sanding is not required at this point.

F = Finished Size: Cut and sand parts to finished size.

Full-Sized Patterns: Set One

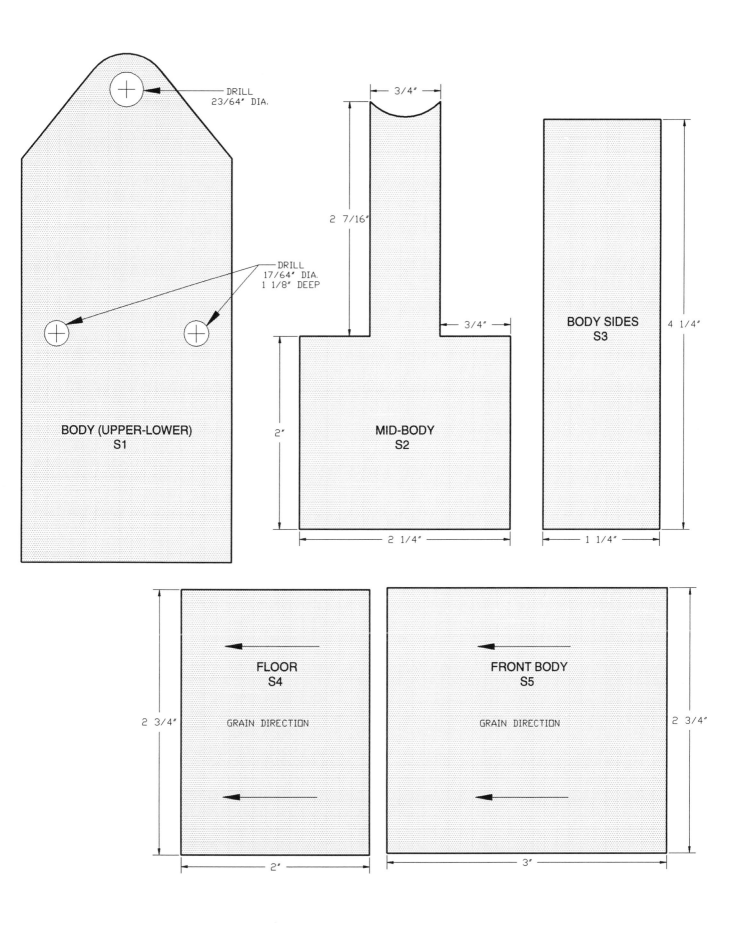

DRILL
23/64" DIA.

DRILL
17/64" DIA.
1 1/8" DEEP

BODY (UPPER-LOWER)
S1

3/4"

2 7/16"

3/4"

2"

MID-BODY
S2

2 1/4"

BODY SIDES
S3

4 1/4"

1 1/4"

FLOOR
S4

GRAIN DIRECTION

2 3/4"

2"

FRONT BODY
S5

GRAIN DIRECTION

2 3/4"

3"

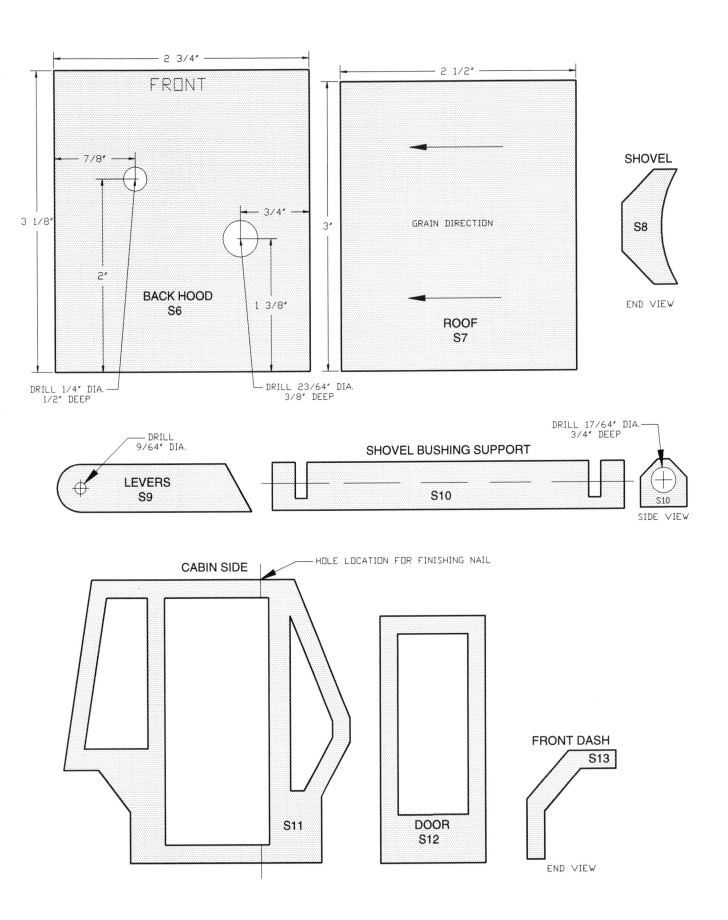

2 3/4"

FRONT

7/8"

3 1/8"

2"

1 3/8"

3/4"

BACK HOOD
S6

DRILL 1/4" DIA.
1/2" DEEP

DRILL 23/64" DIA.
3/8" DEEP

2 1/2"

3"

GRAIN DIRECTION

ROOF
S7

SHOVEL

S8

END VIEW

DRILL
9/64" DIA.

LEVERS
S9

SHOVEL BUSHING SUPPORT

S10

DRILL 17/64" DIA.
3/4" DEEP

S10

SIDE VIEW

CABIN SIDE

HOLE LOCATION FOR FINISHING NAIL

S11

DOOR
S12

FRONT DASH

S13

END VIEW

Skidder: Full-Sized Patterns

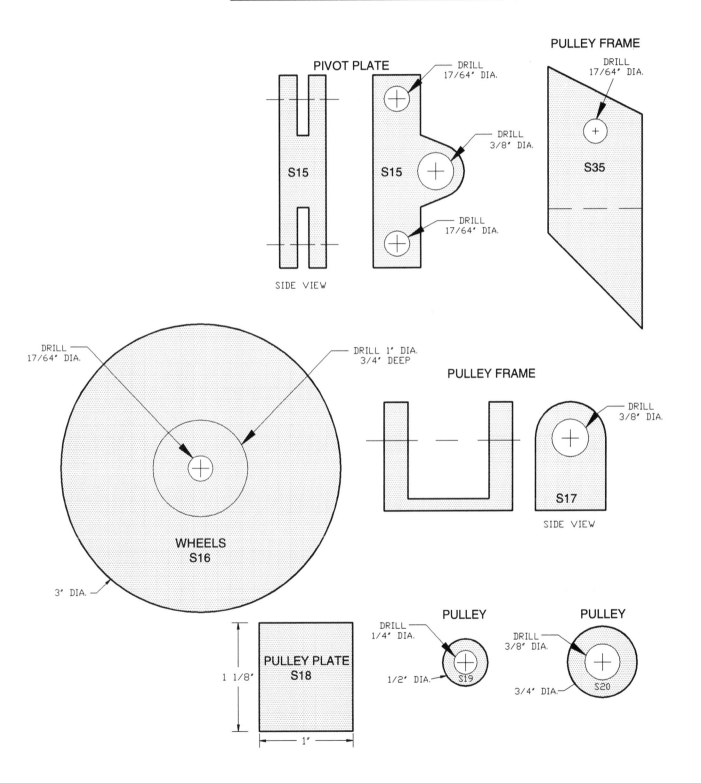

RE-ENFORCING BARS
S14

PIVOT PLATE

PULLEY FRAME

DRILL 17/64" DIA.

S15

S15

DRILL 17/64" DIA.

DRILL 3/8" DIA.

DRILL 17/64" DIA.

SIDE VIEW

DRILL 17/64" DIA.

S35

DRILL 17/64" DIA.

DRILL 1" DIA. 3/4" DEEP

PULLEY FRAME

DRILL 3/8" DIA.

S17

SIDE VIEW

WHEELS
S16

3" DIA.

PULLEY PLATE
S18

1 1/8"

1"

PULLEY

DRILL 1/4" DIA.

1/2" DIA.

S19

PULLEY

DRILL 3/8" DIA.

3/4" DIA.

S20

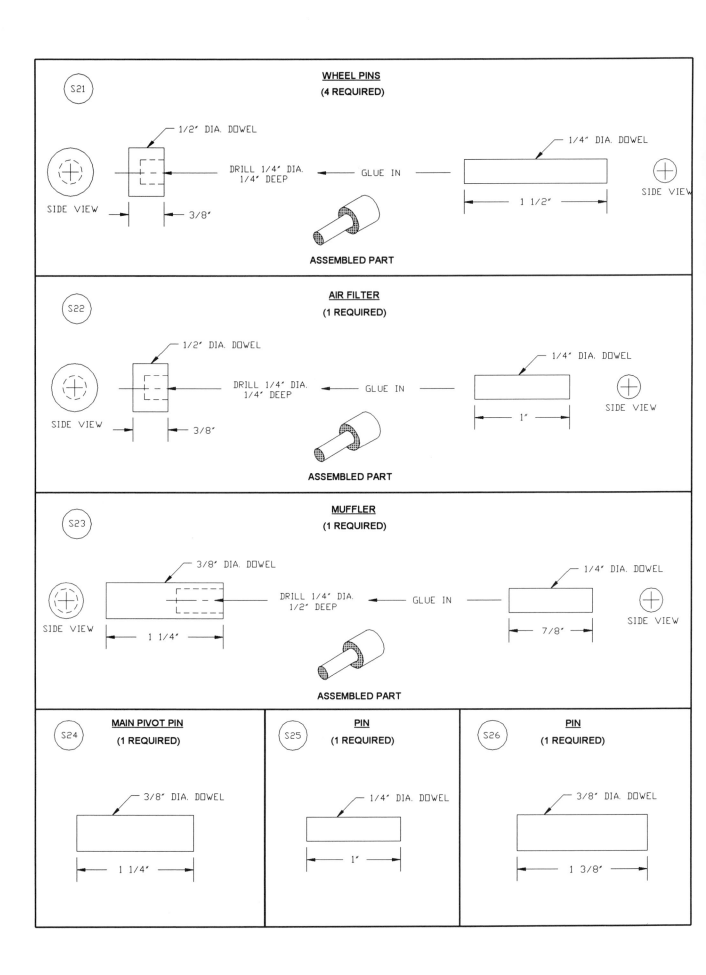

WHEEL PINS
(4 REQUIRED)

S21

1/2″ DIA. DOWEL

DRILL 1/4″ DIA.
1/4″ DEEP

SIDE VIEW

3/8″

GLUE IN

1/4″ DIA. DOWEL

1 1/2″

SIDE VIEW

ASSEMBLED PART

AIR FILTER
(1 REQUIRED)

S22

1/2″ DIA. DOWEL

DRILL 1/4″ DIA.
1/4″ DEEP

SIDE VIEW

3/8″

GLUE IN

1/4″ DIA. DOWEL

1″

SIDE VIEW

ASSEMBLED PART

MUFFLER
(1 REQUIRED)

S23

3/8″ DIA. DOWEL

DRILL 1/4″ DIA.
1/2″ DEEP

SIDE VIEW

1 1/4″

GLUE IN

1/4″ DIA. DOWEL

7/8″

SIDE VIEW

ASSEMBLED PART

MAIN PIVOT PIN
(1 REQUIRED)

S24

3/8″ DIA. DOWEL

1 1/4″

PIN
(1 REQUIRED)

S25

1/4″ DIA. DOWEL

1″

PIN
(1 REQUIRED)

S26

3/8″ DIA. DOWEL

1 3/8″

Skidder: Pins, Shafts, Etc.

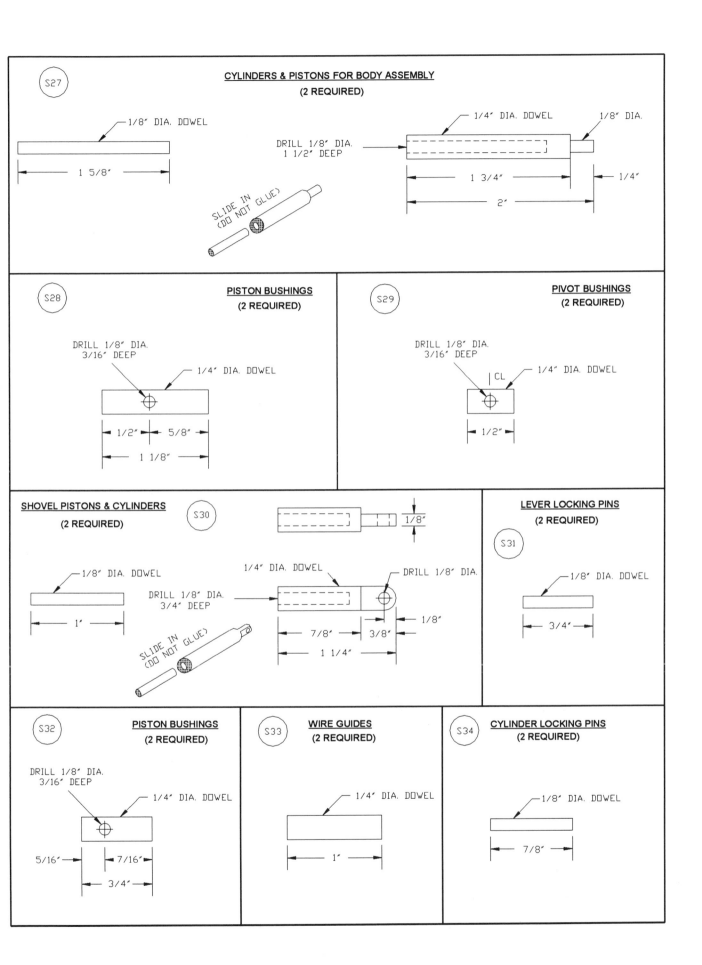

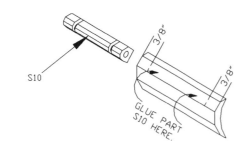

Glue part S10, as shown.

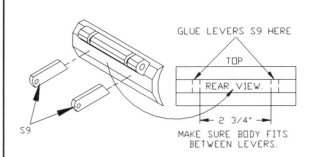

Glue part S9 to shovel, as shown.

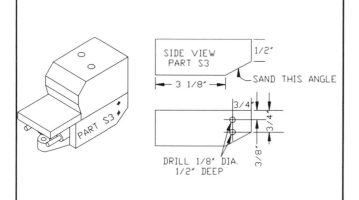

Sand angle and drill holes into sides S3.

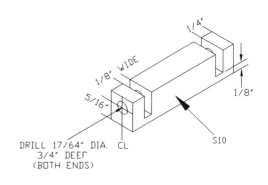

Using your Scroll Saw, cut grooves in part S10.

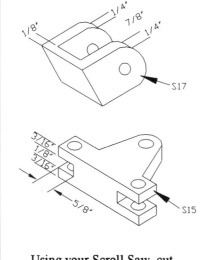

Using your Scroll Saw, cut grooves in part S15 and S17.

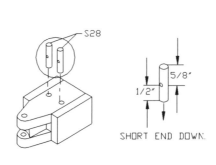

Insert bushings S28 with short end going in first. Do not glue.

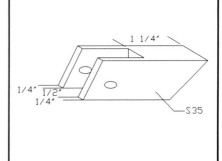

Using your Scroll Saw, cut a groove in part S35, as shown.

Skidder - Assembly Drawings

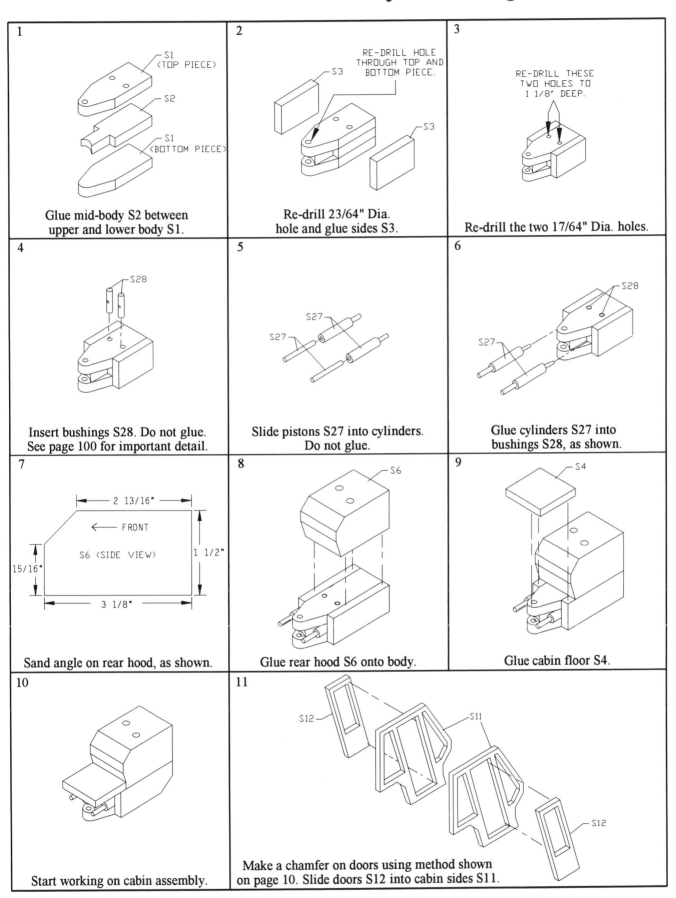

1 Glue mid-body S2 between upper and lower body S1.

2 Re-drill 23/64" Dia. hole and glue sides S3.

3 Re-drill the two 17/64" Dia. holes.

4 Insert bushings S28. Do not glue. See page 100 for important detail.

5 Slide pistons S27 into cylinders. Do not glue.

6 Glue cylinders S27 into bushings S28, as shown.

7 Sand angle on rear hood, as shown.

8 Glue rear hood S6 onto body.

9 Glue cabin floor S4.

10 Start working on cabin assembly.

11 Make a chamfer on doors using method shown on page 10. Slide doors S12 into cabin sides S11.

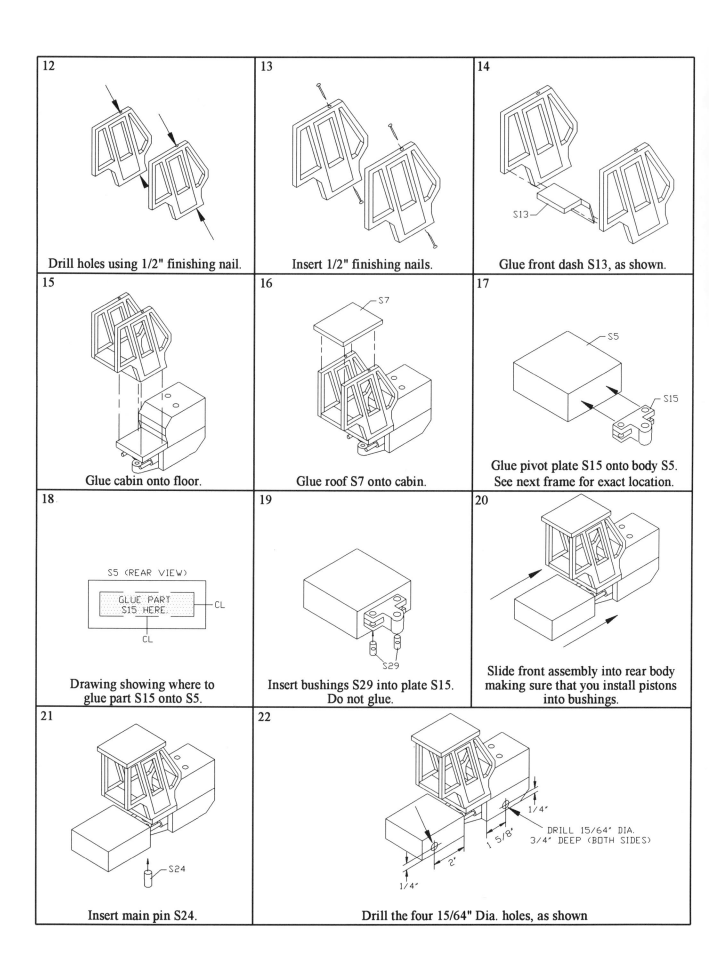

12 Drill holes using 1/2" finishing nail.

13 Insert 1/2" finishing nails.

14 Glue front dash S13, as shown.

15 Glue cabin onto floor.

16 Glue roof S7 onto cabin.

17 Glue pivot plate S15 onto body S5. See next frame for exact location.

18 Drawing showing where to glue part S15 onto S5.

S5 (REAR VIEW)

GLUE PART S15 HERE.

CL

CL

19 Insert bushings S29 into plate S15. Do not glue.

20 Slide front assembly into rear body making sure that you install pistons into bushings.

21 Insert main pin S24.

22 Drill the four 15/64" Dia. holes, as shown

1/4"

5/8"

2"

1/4"

DRILL 15/64" DIA. 3/4" DEEP (BOTH SIDES)

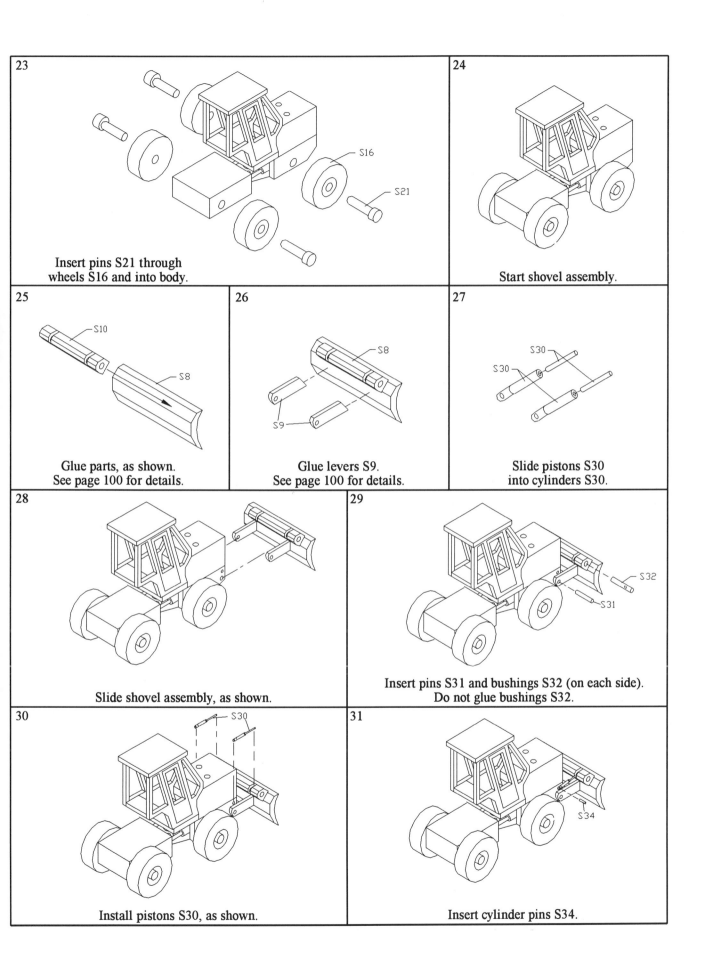

23 Insert pins S21 through wheels S16 and into body.

S16

S21

24 Start shovel assembly.

25 Glue parts, as shown. See page 100 for details.

S10

S8

26 Glue levers S9. See page 100 for details.

S8

S9

27 Slide pistons S30 into cylinders S30.

S30

S30

28 Slide shovel assembly, as shown.

29 Insert pins S31 and bushings S32 (on each side). Do not glue bushings S32.

S32

S31

30 Install pistons S30, as shown.

S30

31 Insert cylinder pins S34.

S34

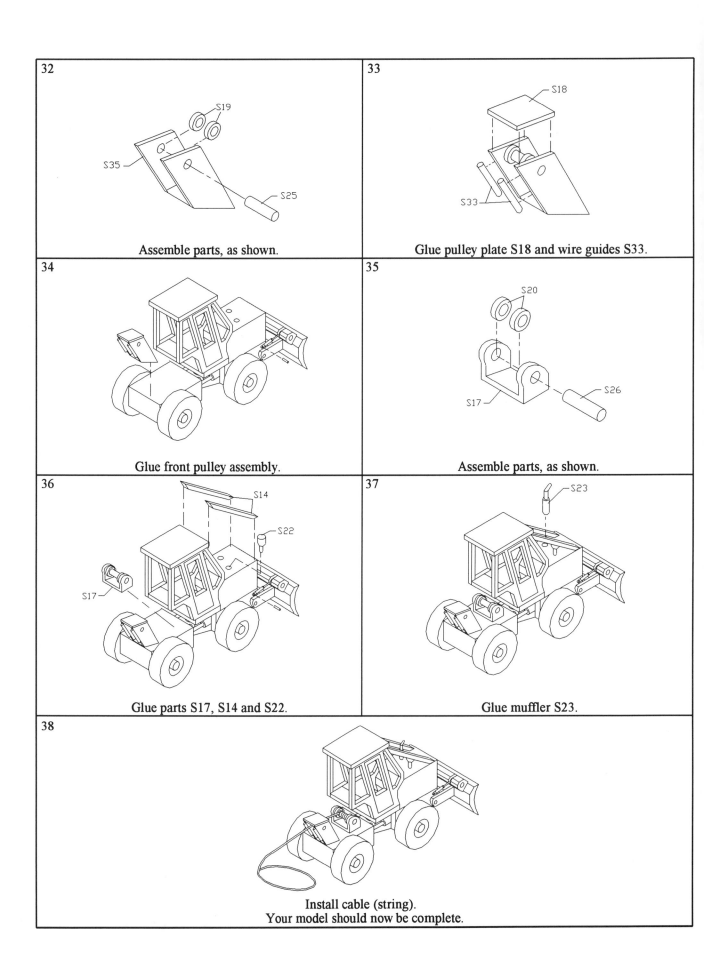

32 Assemble parts, as shown.

33 Glue pulley plate S18 and wire guides S33.

34 Glue front pulley assembly.

35 Assemble parts, as shown.

36 Glue parts S17, S14 and S22.

37 Glue muffler S23.

38 Install cable (string).
Your model should now be complete.

GRAPPLE SKIDDER

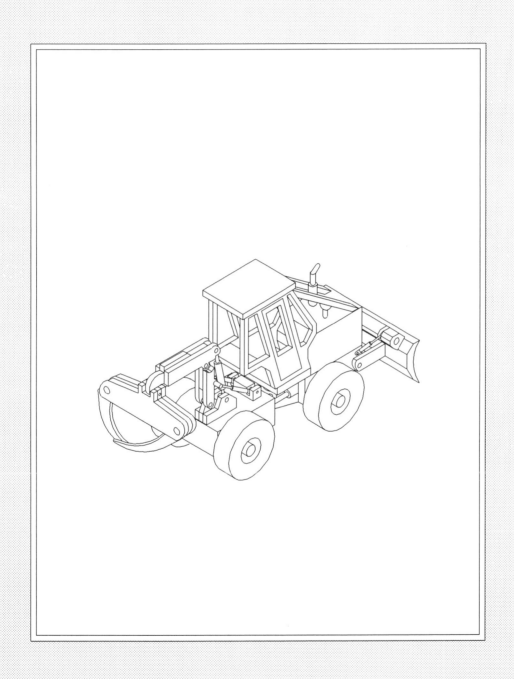

General Instructions - Grapple Skidder

1- Start by cutting materials needed by following the list of materials, paying attention to the rough and finished size. **Identify the parts as they are cut.**

Please note: Different types of wood can be used for the various parts. It is suggested, however, that hard wood be used, since many of the parts would be much too fragile if using soft wood. We have used a combination of pine, maple and oak to give the models a nice contrast!

2- Remove the full-size patterns found in the appendix. Cut them out, leaving approximately 1/16" all around, and place on the proper piece of wood. Patterns can be secured to wood using either spray adhesive or rubber ciment. If using the latter, cut and sand the part first to finished size. If drilling is required, mark the hole by inserting a scriber or nail through the pattern into the wood. Remove the pattern before drilling.

You should have no trouble determining which surface to attach most of the patterns. Some parts, however, can be confusing since the pattern could fit on more than one surface. The drawings below indicate exactly which surface to attach the patterns for these parts.

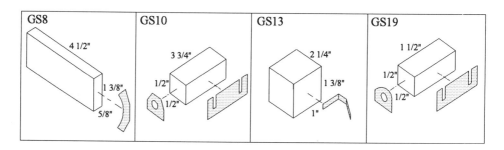

3- Look at the full-size drawing sheets to finish parts GS2, GS6 and GS47.

4- Parts GS10, GS19 and GS36 will need additional cuts and details, please refer to the additional information pages, to complete these parts.

5- Using maple dowels, make all pins, shafts, etc.

6- Follow the assembly drawings to complete your model.

List of Materials - Grapple Skidder

Part	T	W	L	Material	Qty.	*
GS1	3/8"	2 1/2"	5 1/2"	pine	2	R
GS2	1/2"	2 1/4"	4 1/2"	pine	1	F
GS3	1/4"	1 1/4"	4 1/4"	pine	2	F
GS4	1/4"	2 3/4"	2"	pine	1	F
GS5	1 1/4"	2 3/4"	3"	pine	1	F
GS6	1 1/2"	2 3/4"	3 1/8"	pine	1	F
GS7	1/4"	3"	2 1/2"	pine	1	F
GS8	5/8"	1 3/8"	4 1/2"	pine	1	R
GS9	1/4"	3/4"	2 1/4"	maple	2	R
GS10	1/2"	1/2"	3 3/4"	maple	1	F
GS11	1/4"	3 1/4"	3 1/4"	oak	2	R
GS12	1/4"	1 3/8"	2 3/4"	oak	2	R
GS13	1"	1 3/8"	2 1/4"	pine	1	F
GS14	1/4"	2 1/4"	3 1/2"	maple	2	R

Part	T	W	L	Material	Qty.	*
GS15	3/8"	2 1/4"	3 1/2"	maple	1	R
GS16	1/8"	1 5/8"	4"	maple	2	R
GS17	3/16"	1 3/8"	1 3/8"	maple	1	R
GS18	3/16"	1 3/8"	1 3/8"	maple	1	R
GS19	1/2"	1/2"	1 1/2"	maple	1	F
GS20	1/4"	1 3/8"	3 5/8"	maple	2	R
GS21	1/4"	1 3/4"	3 7/8"	maple	1	R
GS22	1/4"	1 1/8"	2 1/8"	maple	2	R
GS23	1/4"	7/8"	2"	maple	1	R
GS24	1/4"	1 1/8"	2"	maple	2	R
GS25	1/4"	1 1/8"	2"	maple	1	R
GS36	1/2"	1 1/8"	2 1/4"	maple	1	R
GS38	1/4"	3/8"	3 3/4"	oak	2	R
GS47	1 1/4"	3" DIA.		oak	4	F

T = Thickness
W = Width
L = Length

R = Rough size
F = Finished size

Instructions:

R= Rough sizes, the material is cut oversized so you have ample room to apply the pattern on the surface. Sanding is not required at this point.

F = Finished Size: Cut and sand parts to finished size.

Full-Sized Patterns: Set One

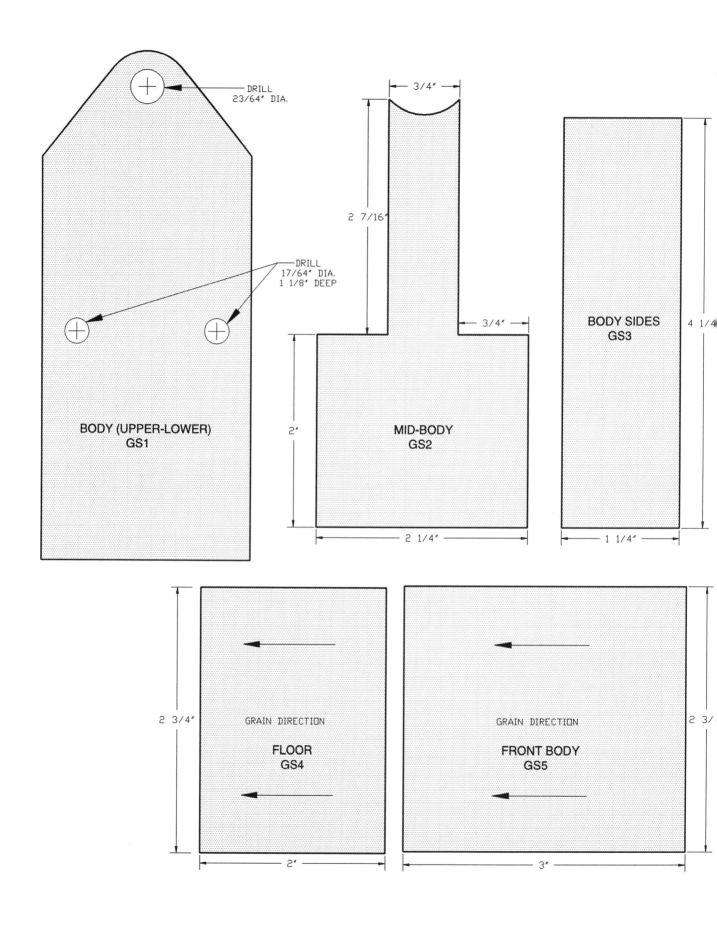

DRILL
23/64" DIA.

DRILL
17/64" DIA.
1 1/8" DEEP

BODY (UPPER-LOWER)
GS1

3/4"

2 7/16"

3/4"

2'

MID-BODY
GS2

2 1/4"

BODY SIDES
GS3

4 1/4"

1 1/4"

2 3/4"

GRAIN DIRECTION

FLOOR
GS4

2'

GRAIN DIRECTION

FRONT BODY
GS5

3'

2 3/

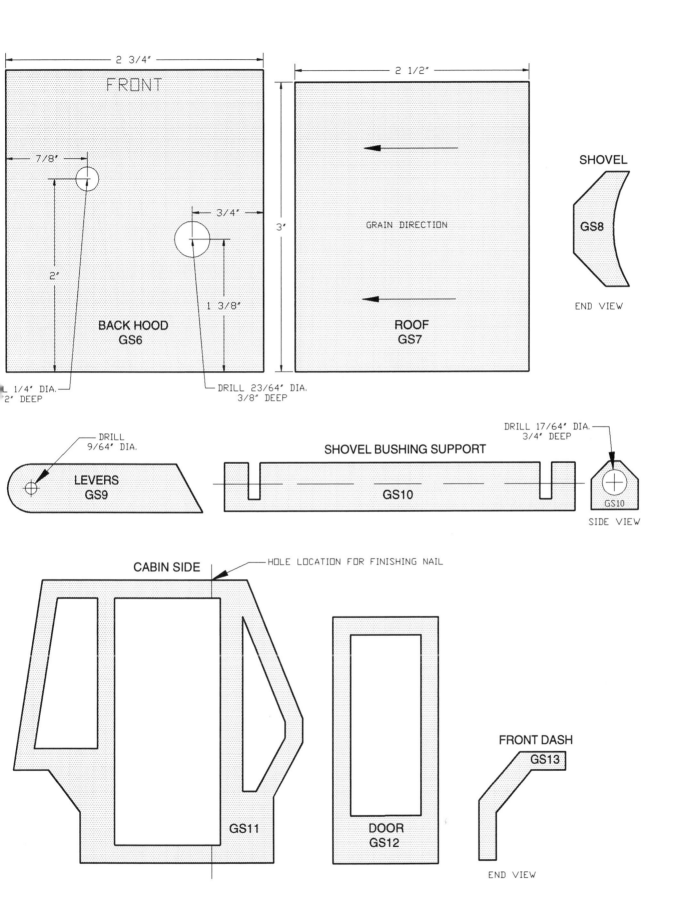

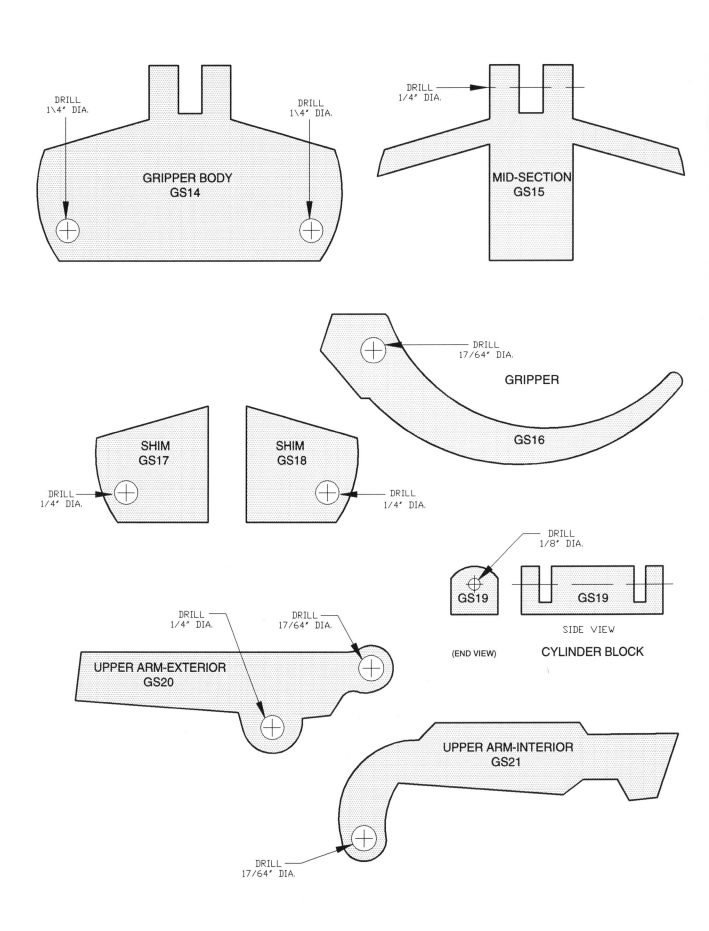

DRILL
1\4″ DIA.

GRIPPER BODY
GS14

DRILL
1\4″ DIA.

DRILL
1/4″ DIA.

MID-SECTION
GS15

DRILL
17/64″ DIA.

GRIPPER

GS16

SHIM
GS17

SHIM
GS18

DRILL
1/4″ DIA.

DRILL
1/4″ DIA.

DRILL
1/8″ DIA.

GS19

GS19

SIDE VIEW

(END VIEW)

CYLINDER BLOCK

DRILL
1/4″ DIA.

DRILL
17/64″ DIA.

UPPER ARM-EXTERIOR
GS20

UPPER ARM-INTERIOR
GS21

DRILL
17/64″ DIA.

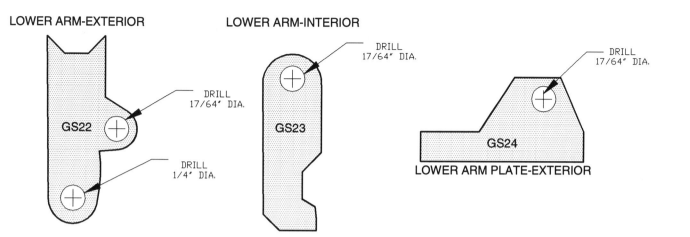

LOWER ARM-EXTERIOR

LOWER ARM-INTERIOR

DRILL 17/64" DIA.

GS22

DRILL 17/64" DIA.

DRILL 1/4" DIA.

GS23

DRILL 17/64" DIA.

GS24

LOWER ARM PLATE-EXTERIOR

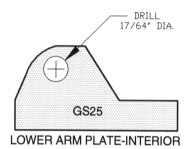

DRILL 17/64" DIA.

GS25

LOWER ARM PLATE-INTERIOR

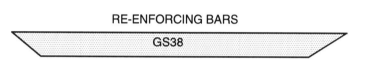

RE-ENFORCING BARS

GS38

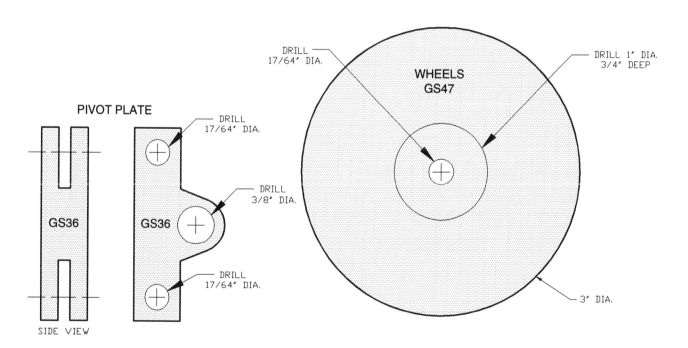

PIVOT PLATE

DRILL 17/64" DIA.

GS36

GS36

DRILL 3/8" DIA.

DRILL 17/64" DIA.

SIDE VIEW

DRILL 17/64" DIA.

WHEELS
GS47

DRILL 1" DIA.
3/4" DEEP

3" DIA.

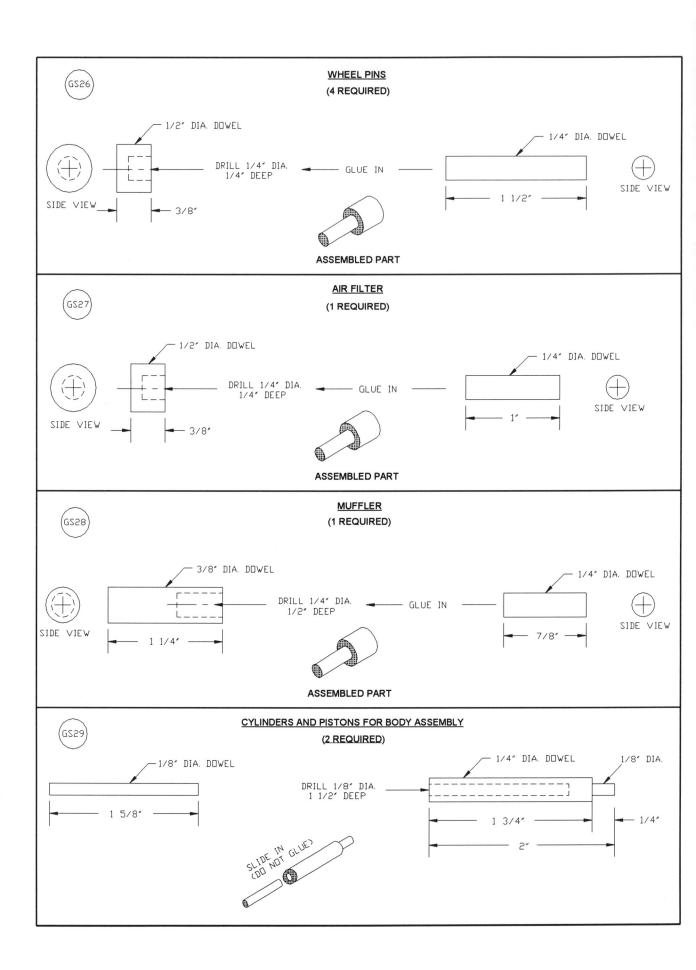

WHEEL PINS
(4 REQUIRED)

GS26

1/2″ DIA. DOWEL

DRILL 1/4″ DIA.
1/4″ DEEP

GLUE IN

1/4″ DIA. DOWEL

SIDE VIEW

3/8″

1 1/2″

SIDE VIEW

ASSEMBLED PART

AIR FILTER
(1 REQUIRED)

GS27

1/2″ DIA. DOWEL

DRILL 1/4″ DIA.
1/4″ DEEP

GLUE IN

1/4″ DIA. DOWEL

SIDE VIEW

3/8″

1″

SIDE VIEW

ASSEMBLED PART

MUFFLER
(1 REQUIRED)

GS28

3/8″ DIA. DOWEL

DRILL 1/4″ DIA.
1/2″ DEEP

GLUE IN

1/4″ DIA. DOWEL

SIDE VIEW

1 1/4″

7/8″

SIDE VIEW

ASSEMBLED PART

CYLINDERS AND PISTONS FOR BODY ASSEMBLY
(2 REQUIRED)

GS29

1/8″ DIA. DOWEL

DRILL 1/8″ DIA.
1 1/2″ DEEP

1/4″ DIA. DOWEL

1/8″ DIA.

1 5/8″

1 3/4″

1/4″

2″

SLIDE IN
(DO NOT GLUE)

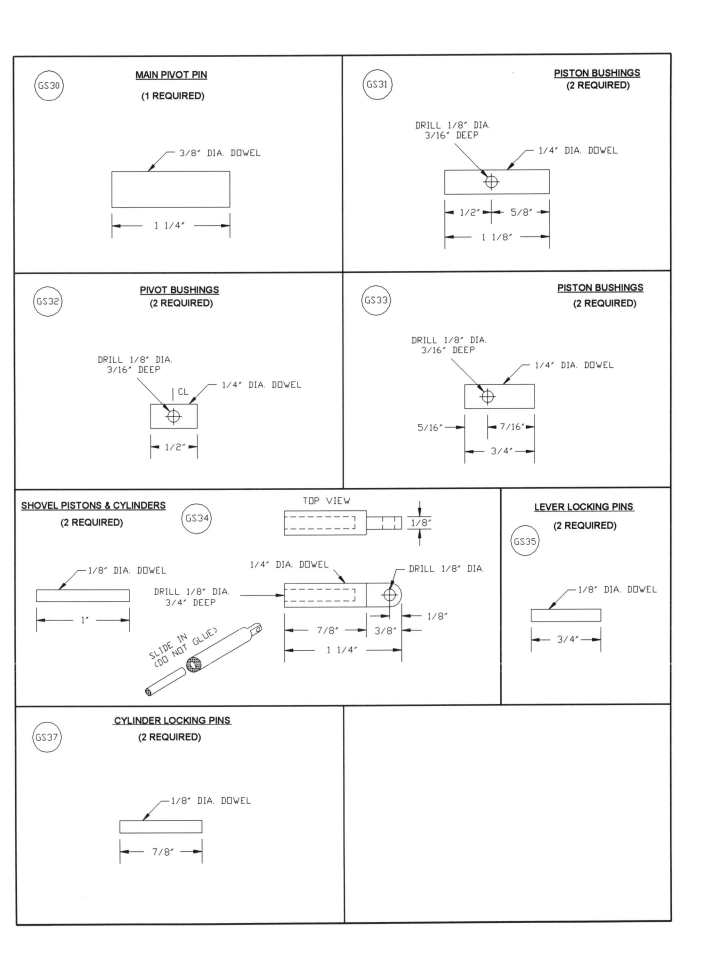

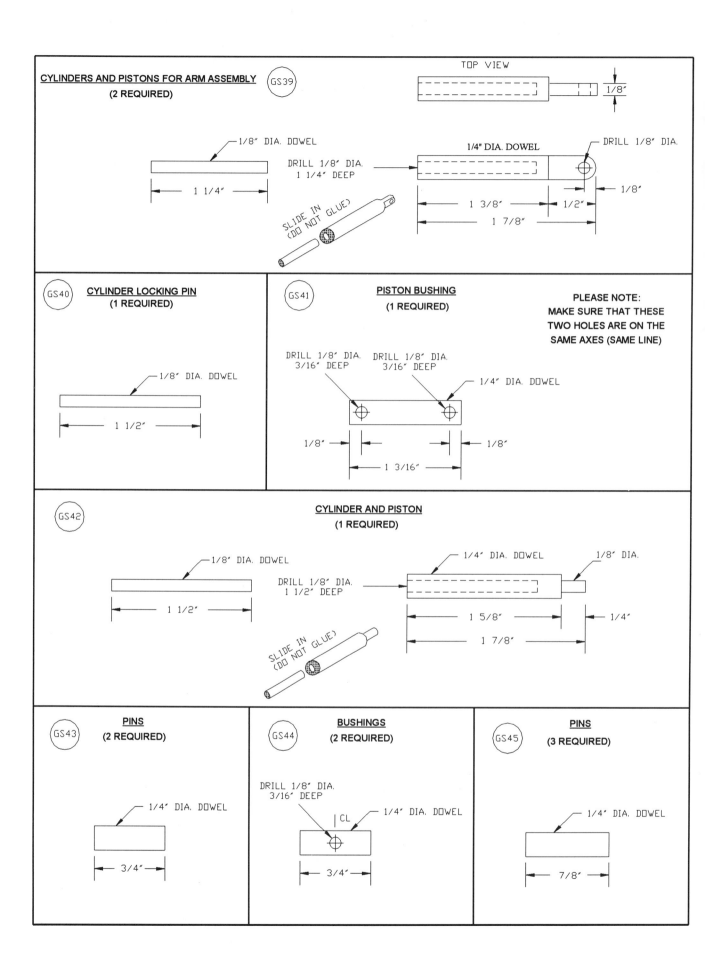

CYLINDERS AND PISTONS FOR ARM ASSEMBLY (GS39)
(2 REQUIRED)

TOP VIEW
1/8″

1/8″ DIA. DOWEL
1 1/4″

DRILL 1/8″ DIA.
1 1/4″ DEEP

1/4″ DIA. DOWEL
DRILL 1/8″ DIA.
1/8″
1 3/8″
1/2″
1 7/8″

SLIDE IN
(DO NOT GLUE)

GS40 CYLINDER LOCKING PIN
(1 REQUIRED)

1/8″ DIA. DOWEL
1 1/2″

GS41 PISTON BUSHING
(1 REQUIRED)

PLEASE NOTE:
MAKE SURE THAT THESE
TWO HOLES ARE ON THE
SAME AXES (SAME LINE)

DRILL 1/8″ DIA.
3/16″ DEEP
DRILL 1/8″ DIA.
3/16″ DEEP
1/4″ DIA. DOWEL
1/8″
1/8″
1 3/16″

GS42 CYLINDER AND PISTON
(1 REQUIRED)

1/8″ DIA. DOWEL
1 1/2″

DRILL 1/8″ DIA.
1 1/2″ DEEP

1/4″ DIA. DOWEL
1/8″ DIA.
1 5/8″
1/4″
1 7/8″

SLIDE IN
(DO NOT GLUE)

GS43 PINS
(2 REQUIRED)

1/4″ DIA. DOWEL
3/4″

GS44 BUSHINGS
(2 REQUIRED)

DRILL 1/8″ DIA.
3/16″ DEEP
CL
1/4″ DIA. DOWEL
3/4″

GS45 PINS
(3 REQUIRED)

1/4″ DIA. DOWEL
7/8″

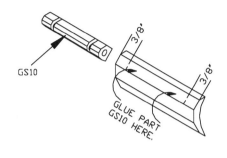

Glue part GS10, as shown.

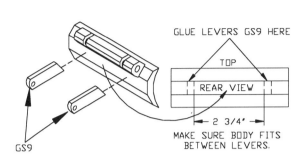

Glue parts GS9 to shovel, as shown.

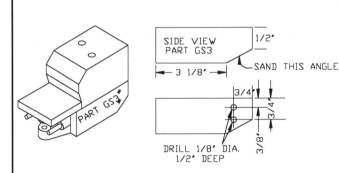

Sand angle and drill 1/8" dia. holes into sides GS3.

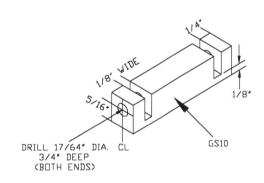

Using your Scroll Saw, cut grooves in part GS10.

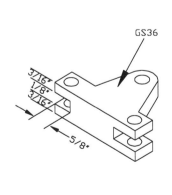

Using your Scroll Saw, cut grooves in part GS36.

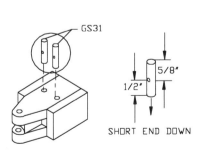

Insert bushings GS31 with short end going in first. Do not glue.

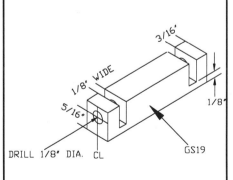

Using your Scroll Saw, cut grooves in part GS19, as shown.

Grapple Skidder - Assembly Drawings

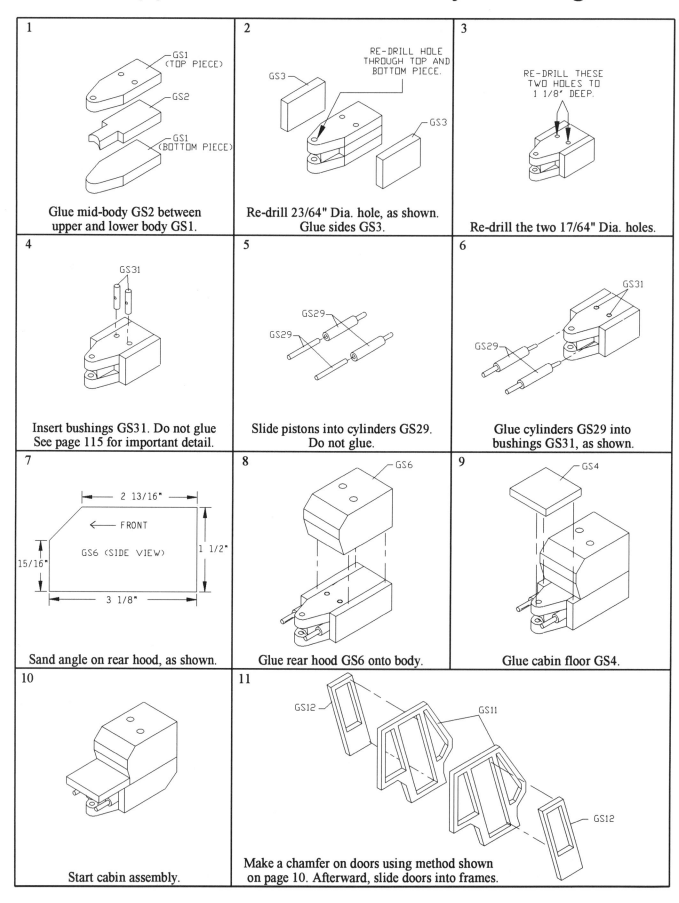

1

GS1 (TOP PIECE)
GS2
GS1 (BOTTOM PIECE)

Glue mid-body GS2 between
upper and lower body GS1.

2

RE-DRILL HOLE THROUGH TOP AND BOTTOM PIECE.
GS3
GS3

Re-drill 23/64" Dia. hole, as shown.
Glue sides GS3.

3

RE-DRILL THESE TWO HOLES TO 1 1/8" DEEP.

Re-drill the two 17/64" Dia. holes.

4

GS31

Insert bushings GS31. Do not glue
See page 115 for important detail.

5

GS29
GS29

Slide pistons into cylinders GS29.
Do not glue.

6

GS31
GS29

Glue cylinders GS29 into
bushings GS31, as shown.

7

2 13/16"
← FRONT
GS6 (SIDE VIEW)
15/16"
1 1/2"
3 1/8"

Sand angle on rear hood, as shown.

8

GS6

Glue rear hood GS6 onto body.

9

GS4

Glue cabin floor GS4.

10

Start cabin assembly.

11

GS12
GS11
GS12

Make a chamfer on doors using method shown
on page 10. Afterward, slide doors into frames.

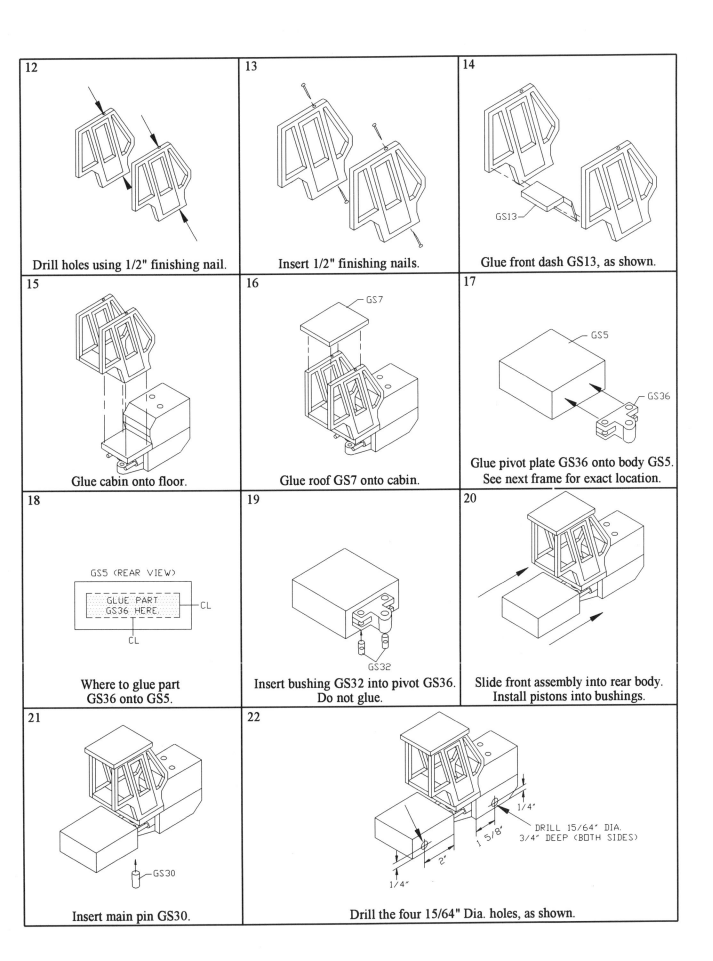

12

Drill holes using 1/2" finishing nail.

13

Insert 1/2" finishing nails.

14

GS13

Glue front dash GS13, as shown.

15

Glue cabin onto floor.

16

GS7

Glue roof GS7 onto cabin.

17

GS5

GS36

Glue pivot plate GS36 onto body GS5.
See next frame for exact location.

18

GS5 (REAR VIEW)

GLUE PART
GS36 HERE.

CL

CL

Where to glue part
GS36 onto GS5.

19

GS32

Insert bushing GS32 into pivot GS36.
Do not glue.

20

Slide front assembly into rear body.
Install pistons into bushings.

21

GS30

Insert main pin GS30.

22

DRILL 15/64" DIA.
3/4" DEEP (BOTH SIDES)

1/4"

1 5/8"

2"

1/4"

Drill the four 15/64" Dia. holes, as shown.

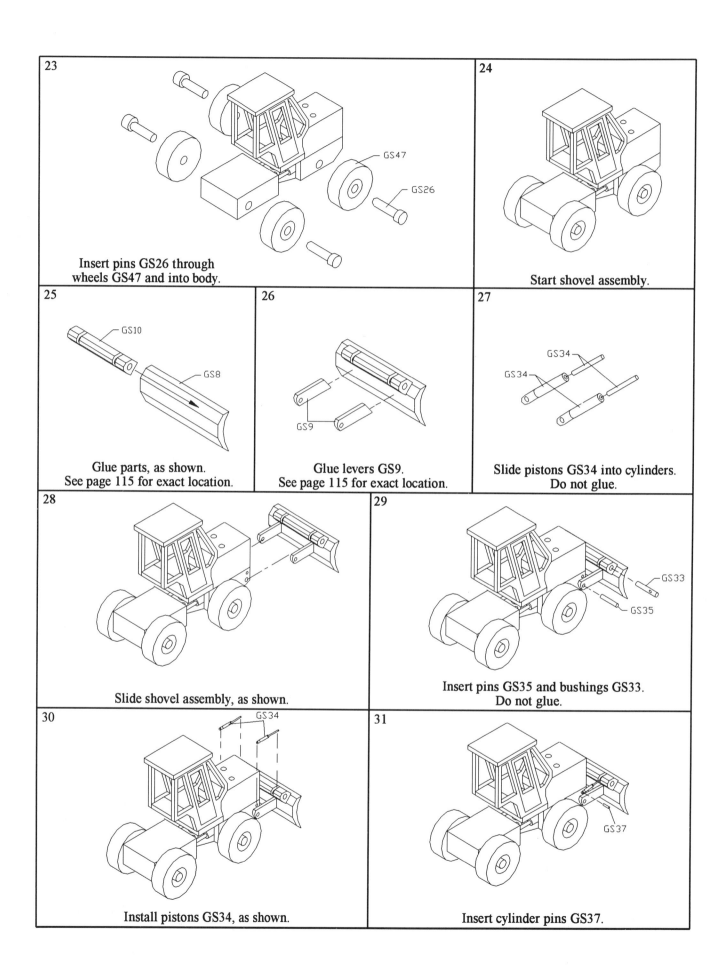

23

Insert pins GS26 through
wheels GS47 and into body.

GS47
GS26

24

Start shovel assembly.

25

GS10
GS8

Glue parts, as shown.
See page 115 for exact location.

26

GS9

Glue levers GS9.
See page 115 for exact location.

27

GS34
GS34

Slide pistons GS34 into cylinders.
Do not glue.

28

Slide shovel assembly, as shown.

29

GS33
GS35

Insert pins GS35 and bushings GS33.
Do not glue.

30

GS34

Install pistons GS34, as shown.

31

GS37

Insert cylinder pins GS37.

Grapple Skidder: Assembly Drawings

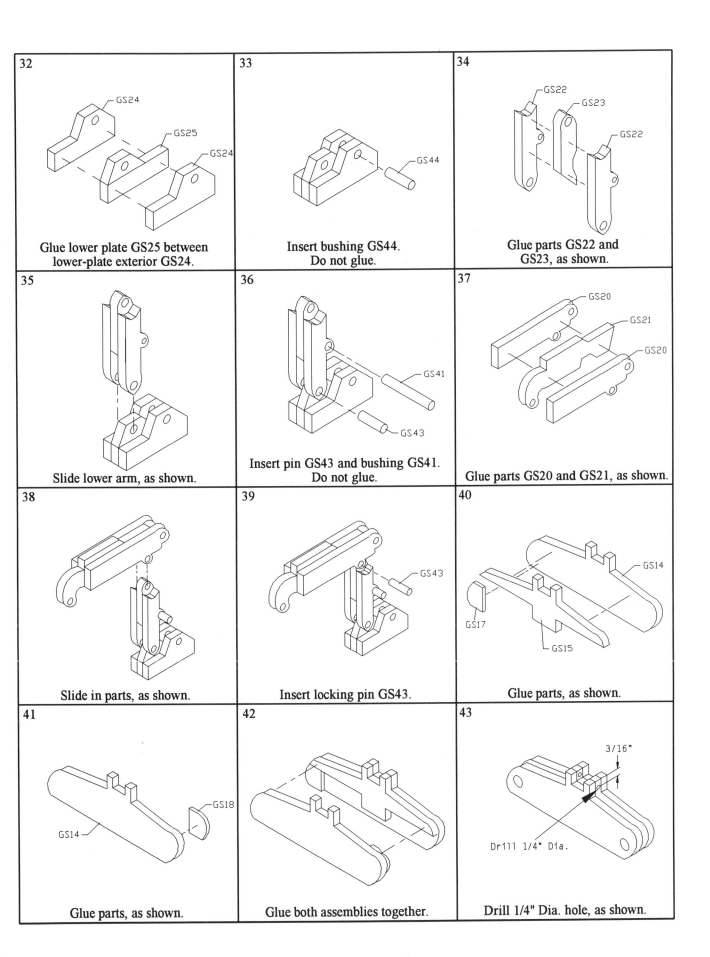

32

Glue lower plate GS25 between
lower-plate exterior GS24.

33

Insert bushing GS44.
Do not glue.

34

Glue parts GS22 and
GS23, as shown.

35

Slide lower arm, as shown.

36

Insert pin GS43 and bushing GS41.
Do not glue.

37

Glue parts GS20 and GS21, as shown.

38

Slide in parts, as shown.

39

Insert locking pin GS43.

40

Glue parts, as shown.

41

Glue parts, as shown.

42

Glue both assemblies together.

43

Drill 1/4" Dia. hole, as shown.

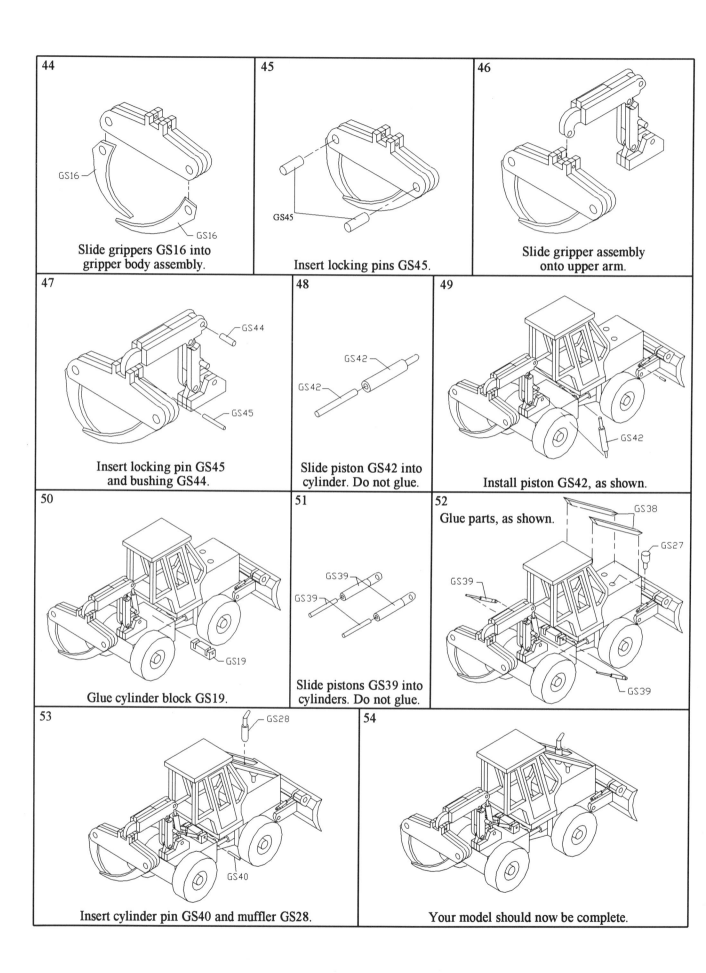

44

GS16

GS16

Slide grippers GS16 into
gripper body assembly.

45

GS45

Insert locking pins GS45.

46

Slide gripper assembly
onto upper arm.

47

GS44

GS45

Insert locking pin GS45
and bushing GS44.

48

GS42

GS42

Slide piston GS42 into
cylinder. Do not glue.

49

GS42

Install piston GS42, as shown.

50

GS19

Glue cylinder block GS19.

51

GS39

GS39

Slide pistons GS39 into
cylinders. Do not glue.

52

Glue parts, as shown.

GS38

GS27

GS39

GS39

53

GS28

GS40

Insert cylinder pin GS40 and muffler GS28.

54

Your model should now be complete.

BACKHOE

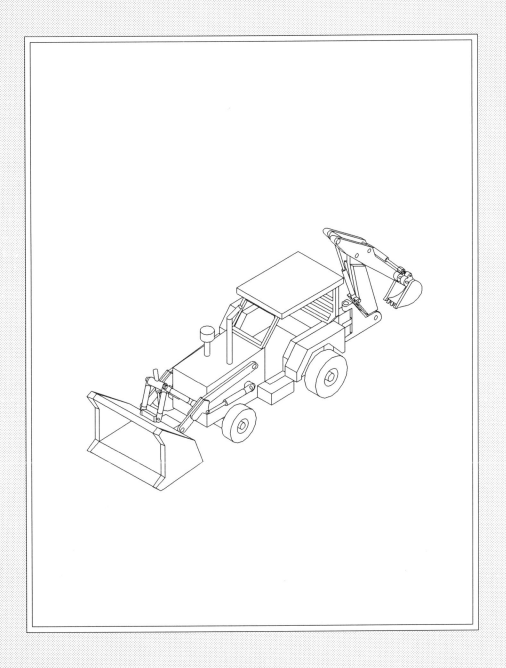

General Instructions - Backhoe

1- Start by cutting materials needed by following the list of materials, paying attention to the rough and finished size. **Identify the parts as they are cut.**

Please note: Different types of wood can be used for the various parts. It is suggested, however, that hard wood be used, since many of the parts would be much too fragile if using soft wood. We have used a combination of pine, maple and oak to give the models a nice contrast!

2- Remove the full-size patterns found in the appendix. Cut them out, leaving approximately 1/16" all around, and place on the proper piece of wood. Patterns can be secured to wood using either spray adhesive or rubber ciment. If using the latter, cut and sand the part first to finished size. If drilling is required, mark the hole by inserting a scriber or nail through the pattern into the wood. Remove the pattern before drilling.

You should have no trouble determining which surface to attach most of the patterns. Some parts, however, can be confusing since the pattern could fit on more than one surface. The drawings below indicate exactly which surface to attach the patterns for these parts.

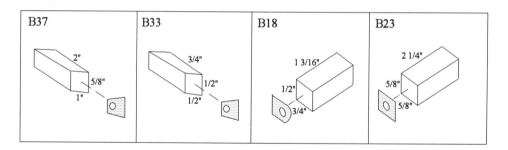

3- Look at the full-size drawing sheets to finish parts B1, B2, B6 and B1B.

4- Parts B13, B16, B18 and B23 will need additional cuts and details, please refer to the additional information pages, to complete these parts.

5- Using maple dowels, make all pins, shafts, etc.

6- Follow the assembly drawings to complete your model.

List of Materials - Backhoe

Part	T	W	L	Material	Qty.	*
B1	1 1/2"	1 3/4"	3 1/4"	pine	1	F
B1A	3/4"	1 3/4"	6"	pine	1	F
B1B	1/4"	3/4"	2 3/4"	pine	2	F
B2	1/2"	2 1/4"	1 3/4"	pine	1	F
B3	3/4"	1 1/8"	2 7/8"	pine	2	R
B4	1/4"	3 1/4"	4"	oak	2	R
B5	1/4"	1 1/4"	2 1/2"	oak	2	R
B7	1/4"	2 3/4"	3 1/2"	pine	1	F
B8	1/4"	2"	2 1/4"	pine	2	R
B9	3/4"	1 1/4"	1 1/8"	oak	2	R
B10	1/4"	1 5/8"	3 3/4"	pine	1	F
B11	1/4"	2 1/8"	3 3/4"	pine	1	F
B12	1/8"	1 1/4"	4 3/8"	pine	1	R
B13	3/4"	1 7/8"	2 1/8"	maple	1	R

Part	T	W	L	Material	Qty.	*
B14	1/4"	1 1/8"	5 1/8"	maple	2	R
B15	1/8"	1 1/8"	1 3/4"	maple	4	R
B16	1"	1 5/8"	2 1/2"	maple	1	R
B17	1/4"	1 5/8"	2 1/8"	maple	2	R
B18	1/2"	3/4"	1 3/16"	maple	1	F
B19	1/4"	1 3/8"	4"	maple	2	R
B20	1/4"	1 1/8"	4 1/4"	maple	1	R
B21	1"	2 1/2" DIA.		oak	2	F
B22	3/4"	1 1/2" DIA.		oak	2	F
B23	5/8"	5/8"	2 1/4"	maple	1	F
B23A	1/4"	1 1/4"	3 3/4"	maple	2	R
B24	1/4"	1 1/8"	5"	maple	1	R
B37	5/8"	1"	2"	maple	1	F
B52	1/2"	1/2"	3/4"	maple	1	F

T = Thickness
W = Width
L = Length

R = Rough size
F = Finished size

Instructions:

R= Rough sizes, the material is cut oversized so you have ample room to apply the pattern on the surface. Sanding is not required at this point.

F = Finished Size: Cut and sand parts to finished size.

Full-Sized Patterns: Set One

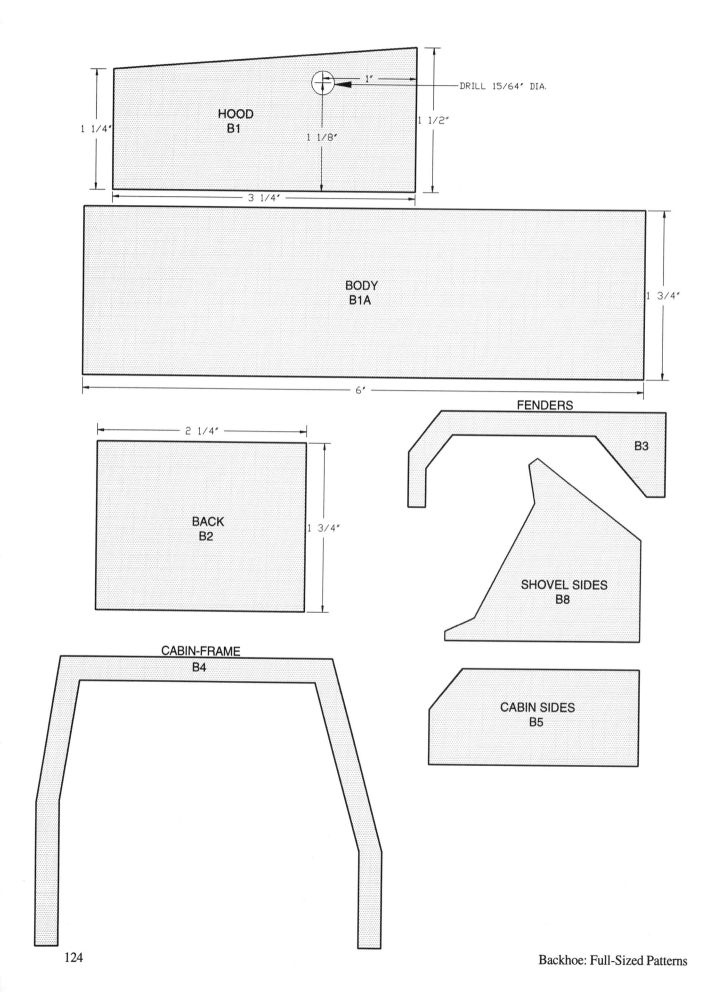

HOOD
B1

1 1/4"

1 1/8"

DRILL 15/64" DIA.

1"

1 1/2"

3 1/4"

BODY
B1A

1 3/4"

6"

2 1/4"

BACK
B2

1 3/4"

FENDERS

B3

SHOVEL SIDES
B8

CABIN-FRAME
B4

CABIN SIDES
B5

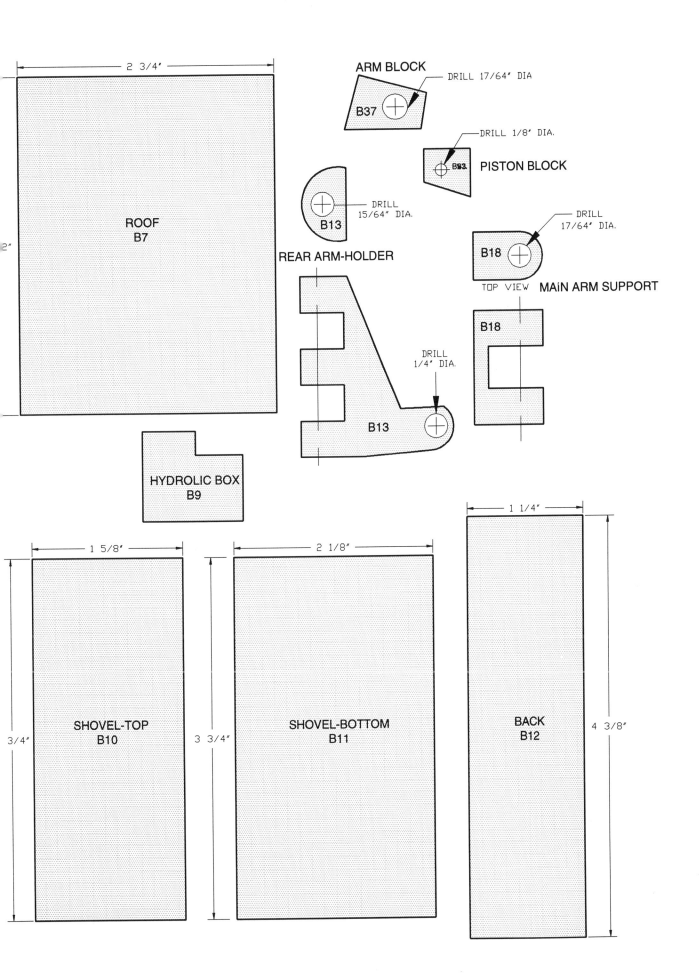

2 3/4'

ROOF
B7

2"

ARM BLOCK

DRILL 17/64" DIA

B37

DRILL 1/8' DIA.

B93. PISTON BLOCK

DRILL
15/64" DIA.

B13

REAR ARM-HOLDER

DRILL
17/64' DIA.

B18

TOP VIEW   MAIN ARM SUPPORT

B18

DRILL
1/4' DIA.

B13

HYDROLIC BOX
B9

1 5/8'

3/4"

SHOVEL-TOP
B10

2 1/8'

3 3/4'

SHOVEL-BOTTOM
B11

1 1/4'

BACK
B12

4 3/8"

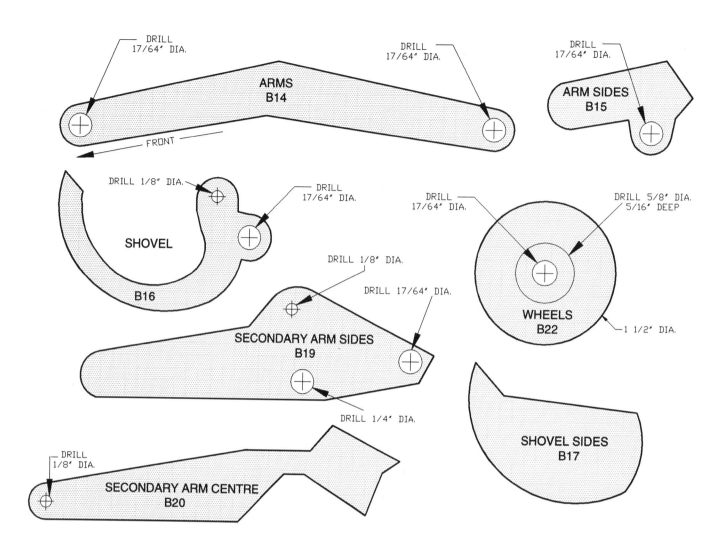

DRILL 17/64" DIA.

DRILL 17/64" DIA.

DRILL 17/64" DIA.

ARMS
B14

FRONT

ARM SIDES
B15

DRILL 1/8" DIA.

DRILL 17/64" DIA.

SHOVEL

B16

DRILL 1/8" DIA.

DRILL 17/64" DIA.

DRILL 17/64" DIA.

DRILL 5/8" DIA.
5/16" DEEP

SECONDARY ARM SIDES
B19

WHEELS
B22

1 1/2" DIA.

DRILL 1/4" DIA.

DRILL 1/8" DIA.

SECONDARY ARM CENTRE
B20

SHOVEL SIDES
B17

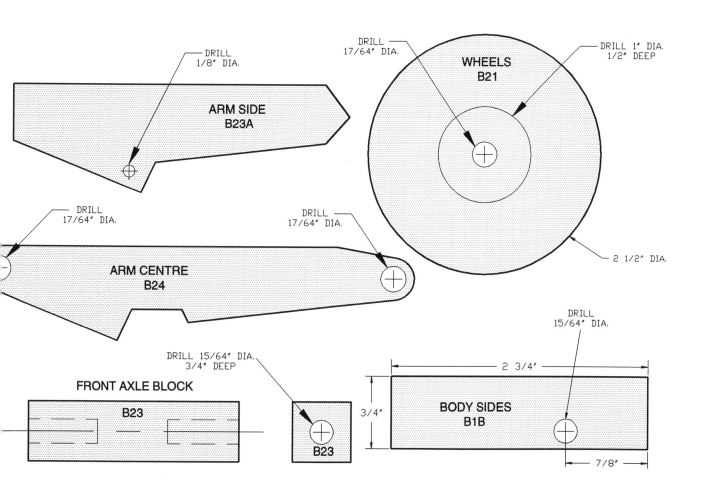

DRILL
1/8″ DIA.

ARM SIDE
B23A

DRILL
17/64″ DIA.

WHEELS
B21

DRILL 1″ DIA.
1/2″ DEEP

DRILL
17/64″ DIA.

DRILL
17/64″ DIA.

ARM CENTRE
B24

2 1/2″ DIA.

DRILL 15/64″ DIA.
3/4″ DEEP

FRONT AXLE BLOCK

B23

B23

DRILL
15/64″ DIA.

2 3/4″

3/4″

BODY SIDES
B1B

7/8″

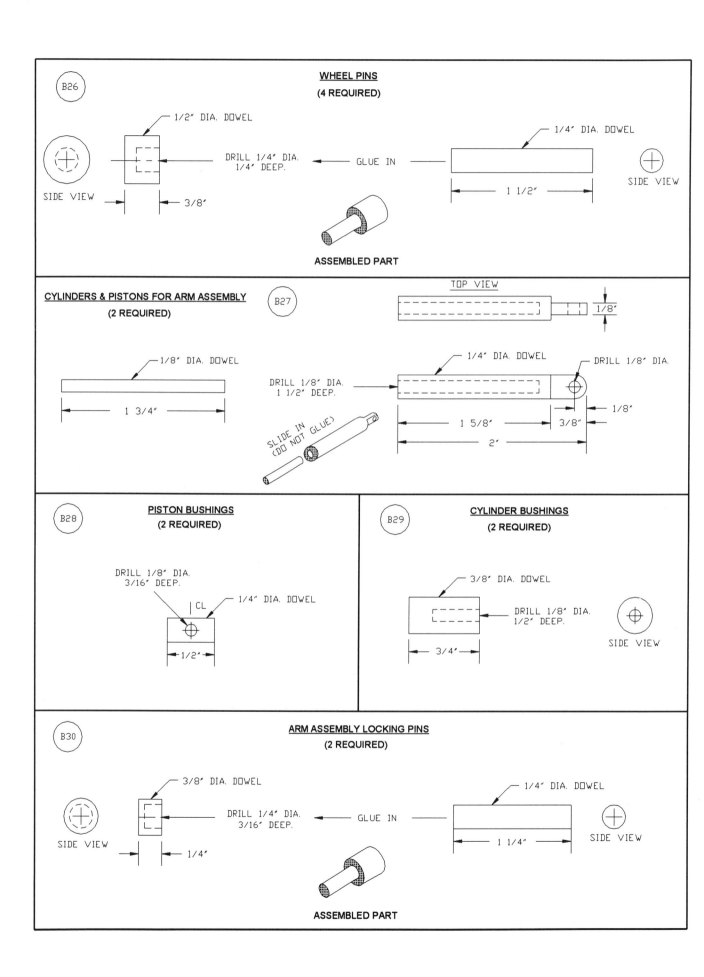

WHEEL PINS
(4 REQUIRED)

B26

1/2″ DIA. DOWEL

SIDE VIEW

DRILL 1/4″ DIA.
1/4″ DEEP.

3/8″

GLUE IN

1/4″ DIA. DOWEL

1 1/2″

SIDE VIEW

ASSEMBLED PART

CYLINDERS & PISTONS FOR ARM ASSEMBLY
(2 REQUIRED)

B27

TOP VIEW

1/8″

1/8″ DIA. DOWEL

1 3/4″

DRILL 1/8″ DIA.
1 1/2″ DEEP.

1/4″ DIA. DOWEL

DRILL 1/8″ DIA.

1/8″

1 5/8″

3/8″

2″

SLIDE IN
(DO NOT GLUE)

PISTON BUSHINGS
(2 REQUIRED)

B28

DRILL 1/8″ DIA.
3/16″ DEEP.

CL

1/4″ DIA. DOWEL

1/2″

CYLINDER BUSHINGS
(2 REQUIRED)

B29

3/8″ DIA. DOWEL

DRILL 1/8″ DIA.
1/2″ DEEP.

SIDE VIEW

3/4″

ARM ASSEMBLY LOCKING PINS
(2 REQUIRED)

B30

3/8″ DIA. DOWEL

SIDE VIEW

DRILL 1/4″ DIA.
3/16″ DEEP.

1/4″

GLUE IN

1/4″ DIA. DOWEL

1 1/4″

SIDE VIEW

ASSEMBLED PART

Backhoe: Pins, Shafts, Etc.

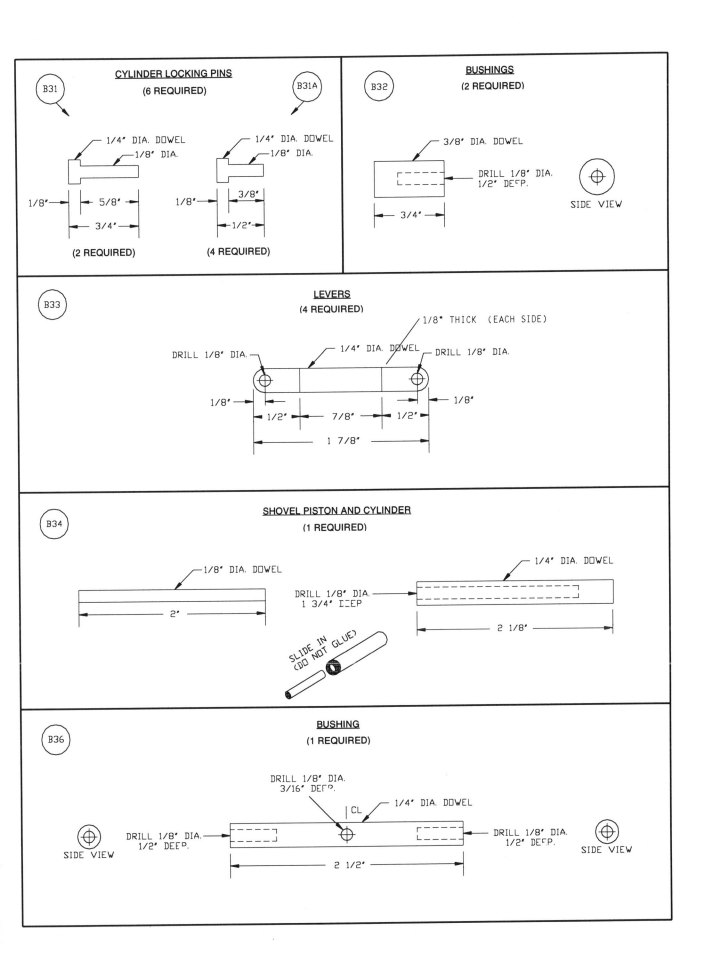

CYLINDER LOCKING PINS
(6 REQUIRED)

B31

B31A

1/4" DIA. DOWEL
1/8" DIA.

1/8"
5/8"
3/4"

(2 REQUIRED)

1/4" DIA. DOWEL
1/8" DIA.

1/8"
3/8"
1/2"

(4 REQUIRED)

BUSHINGS
(2 REQUIRED)

B32

3/8" DIA. DOWEL

DRILL 1/8" DIA.
1/2" DEEP.

3/4"

SIDE VIEW

LEVERS
(4 REQUIRED)

B33

1/8" THICK (EACH SIDE)

DRILL 1/8" DIA.

1/4" DIA. DOWEL

DRILL 1/8" DIA.

1/8"

1/8"

1/2"
7/8"
1/2"

1 7/8"

SHOVEL PISTON AND CYLINDER
(1 REQUIRED)

B34

1/8" DIA. DOWEL

2"

DRILL 1/8" DIA.
1 3/4" DEEP

1/4" DIA. DOWEL

2 1/8"

SLIDE IN
(DO NOT GLUE)

BUSHING
(1 REQUIRED)

B36

DRILL 1/8" DIA.
3/16" DEEP.

CL

1/4" DIA. DOWEL

DRILL 1/8" DIA.
1/2" DEEP.

DRILL 1/8" DIA.
1/2" DEEP.

SIDE VIEW

SIDE VIEW

2 1/2"

Backhoe: Pins, Shafts, Etc.

129

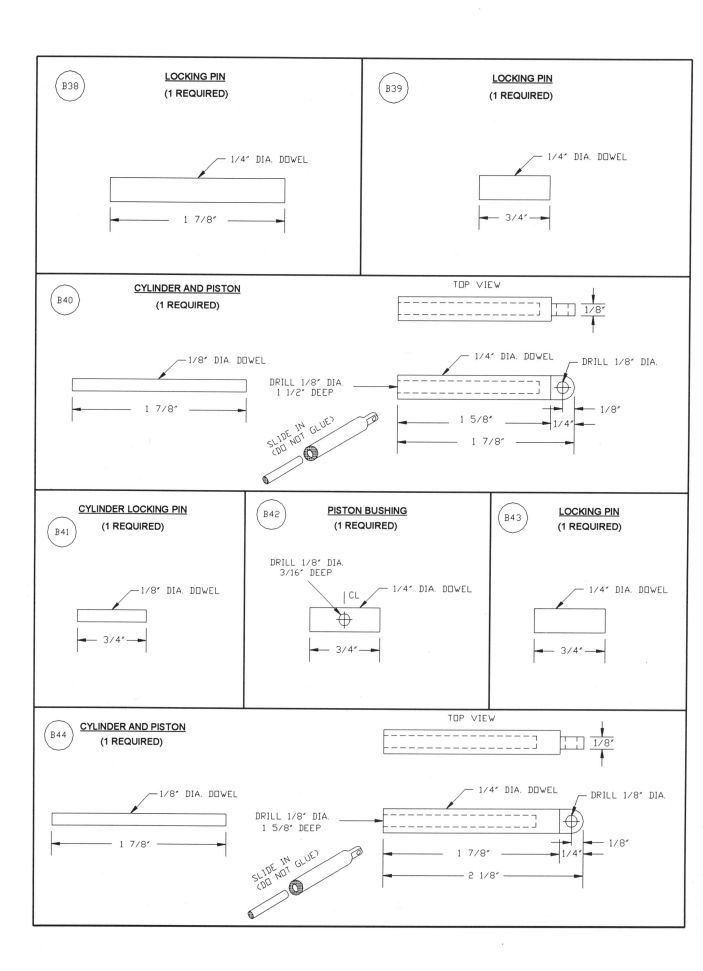

B38   **LOCKING PIN**
(1 REQUIRED)

1/4″ DIA. DOWEL

1 7/8″

B39   **LOCKING PIN**
(1 REQUIRED)

1/4″ DIA. DOWEL

3/4″

B40   **CYLINDER AND PISTON**
(1 REQUIRED)

TOP VIEW

1/8″

1/8″ DIA. DOWEL

1 7/8″

DRILL 1/8″ DIA.
1 1/2″ DEEP

SLIDE IN
(DO NOT GLUE)

1/4″ DIA. DOWEL

DRILL 1/8″ DIA.

1 5/8″

1/8″

1/4″

1 7/8″

B41   **CYLINDER LOCKING PIN**
(1 REQUIRED)

1/8″ DIA. DOWEL

3/4″

B42   **PISTON BUSHING**
(1 REQUIRED)

DRILL 1/8″ DIA.
3/16″ DEEP

CL

1/4″ DIA. DOWEL

3/4″

B43   **LOCKING PIN**
(1 REQUIRED)

1/4″ DIA. DOWEL

3/4″

B44   **CYLINDER AND PISTON**
(1 REQUIRED)

TOP VIEW

1/8″

1/8″ DIA. DOWEL

1 7/8″

DRILL 1/8″ DIA.
1 5/8″ DEEP

SLIDE IN
(DO NOT GLUE)

1/4″ DIA. DOWEL

DRILL 1/8″ DIA.

1 7/8″

1/8″

1/4″

2 1/8″

Backhoe: Pins, Shafts, Etc.

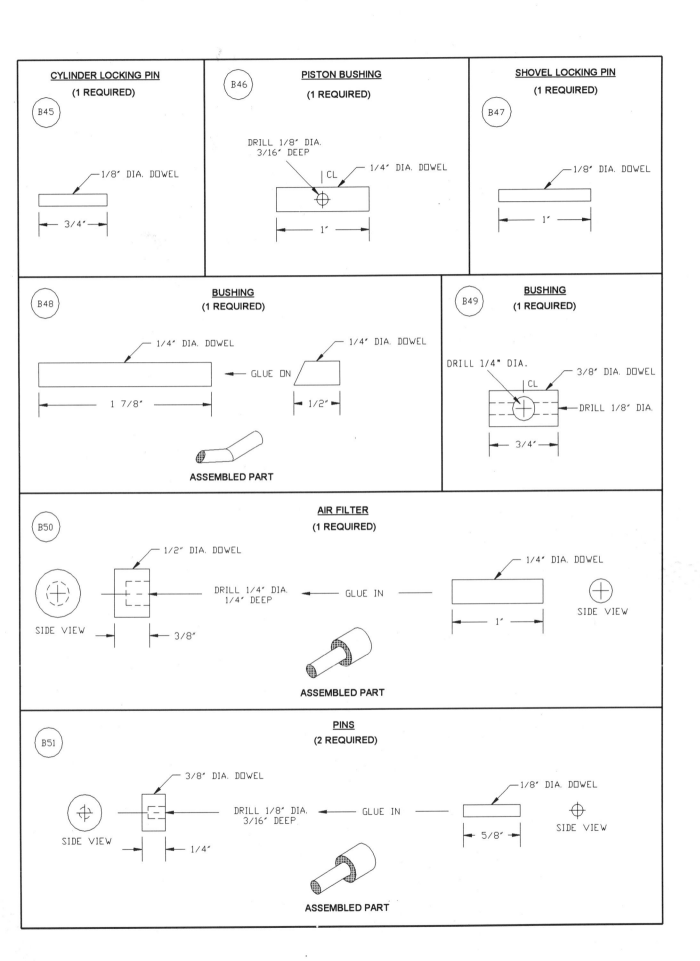

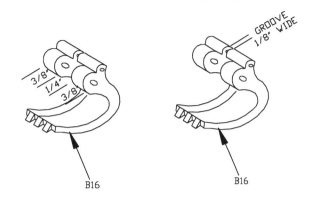

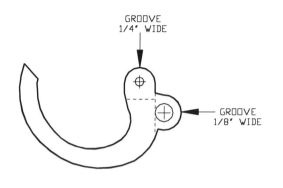

Using your Scroll Saw, cut grooves in part B16, as shown.

Additional details - grooves.

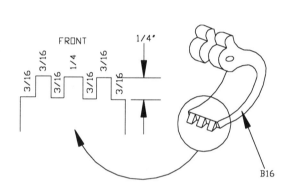

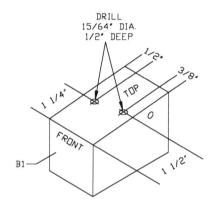

Using your Scroll Saw, cut grooves, as shown.

Drill holes into body B1, as shown.

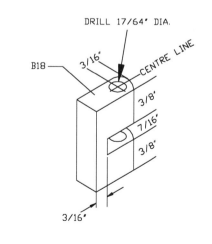

Important: When you cut this groove, make sure that arm assembly fits in tight. (this way, arm assembly stays up)

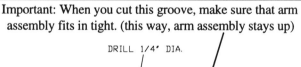

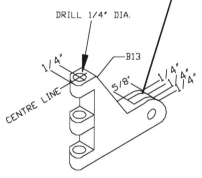

Using your Scroll Saw, cut groove in part B18, as shown.

Using your Scroll Saw, cut grooves in part B13, as shown.

Backhoe - Assembly Drawings

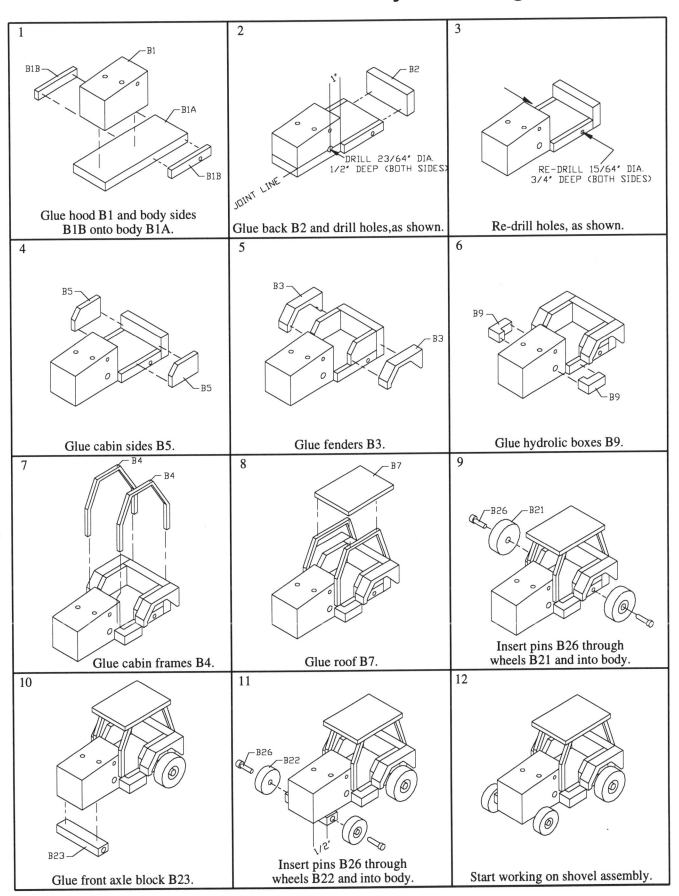

1 Glue hood B1 and body sides B1B onto body B1A.

2 Glue back B2 and drill holes, as shown.

DRILL 23/64" DIA. 1/2" DEEP (BOTH SIDES)

JOINT LINE

3 Re-drill holes, as shown.

RE-DRILL 15/64" DIA. 3/4" DEEP (BOTH SIDES)

4 Glue cabin sides B5.

5 Glue fenders B3.

6 Glue hydrolic boxes B9.

7 Glue cabin frames B4.

8 Glue roof B7.

9 Insert pins B26 through wheels B21 and into body.

10 Glue front axle block B23.

11 Insert pins B26 through wheels B22 and into body.

12 Start working on shovel assembly.

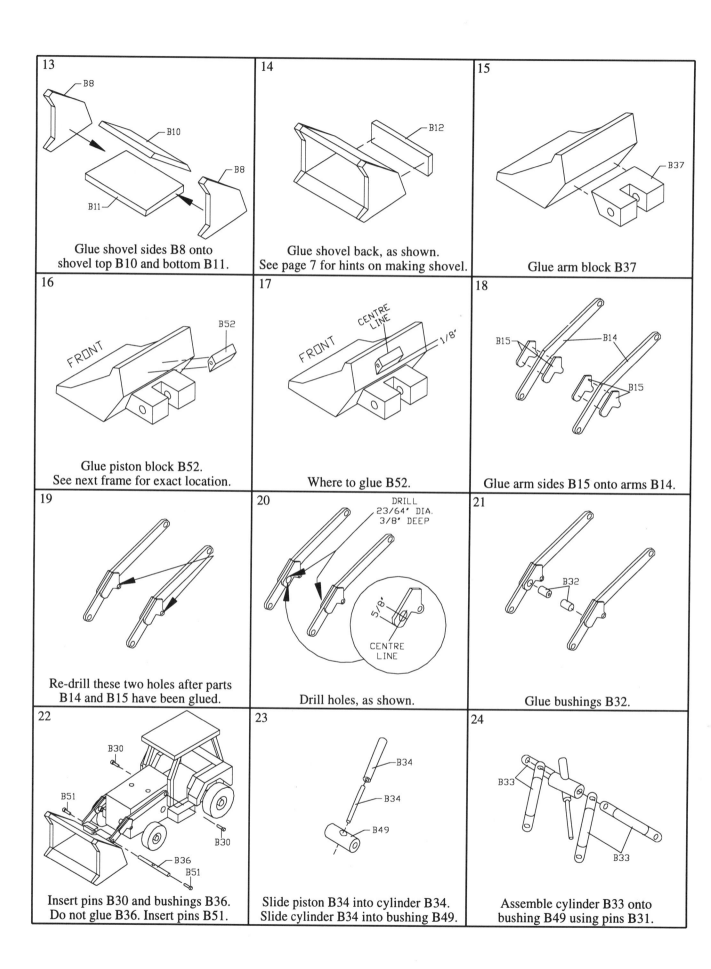

13 Glue shovel sides B8 onto shovel top B10 and bottom B11.

14 Glue shovel back, as shown. See page 7 for hints on making shovel.

15 Glue arm block B37

16 Glue piston block B52. See next frame for exact location.

17 Where to glue B52.

18 Glue arm sides B15 onto arms B14.

19 Re-drill these two holes after parts B14 and B15 have been glued.

20 Drill holes, as shown.

DRILL 23/64" DIA. 3/8" DEEP

21 Glue bushings B32.

22 Insert pins B30 and bushings B36. Do not glue B36. Insert pins B51.

23 Slide piston B34 into cylinder B34. Slide cylinder B34 into bushing B49.

24 Assemble cylinder B33 onto bushing B49 using pins B31.

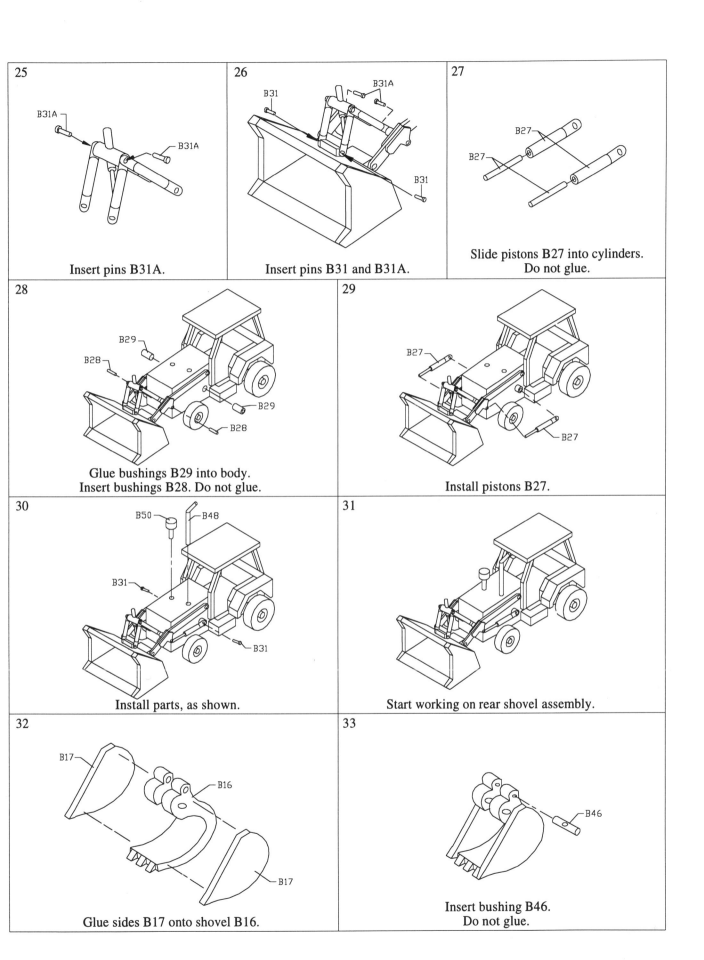

25

Insert pins B31A.

26

Insert pins B31 and B31A.

27

Slide pistons B27 into cylinders.
Do not glue.

28

Glue bushings B29 into body.
Insert bushings B28. Do not glue.

29

Install pistons B27.

30

Install parts, as shown.

31

Start working on rear shovel assembly.

32

Glue sides B17 onto shovel B16.

33

Insert bushing B46.
Do not glue.

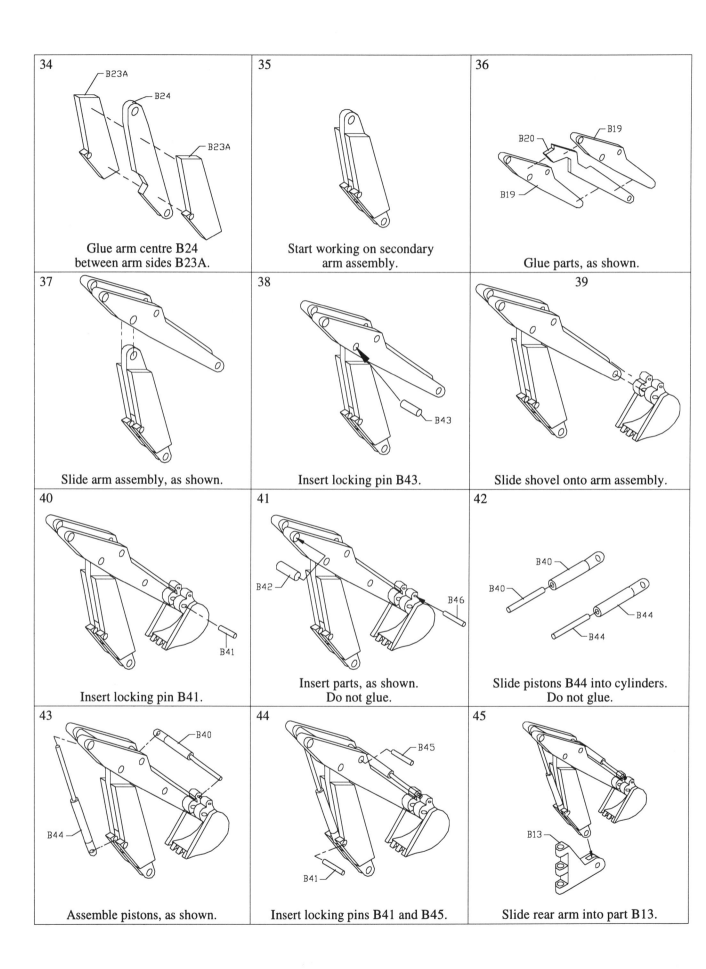

34 Glue arm centre **B24** between arm sides **B23A**.

35 Start working on secondary arm assembly.

36 Glue parts, as shown.

37 Slide arm assembly, as shown.

38 Insert locking pin B43.

39 Slide shovel onto arm assembly.

40 Insert locking pin B41.

41 Insert parts, as shown. Do not glue.

42 Slide pistons B44 into cylinders. Do not glue.

43 Assemble pistons, as shown.

44 Insert locking pins B41 and B45.

45 Slide rear arm into part **B13**.

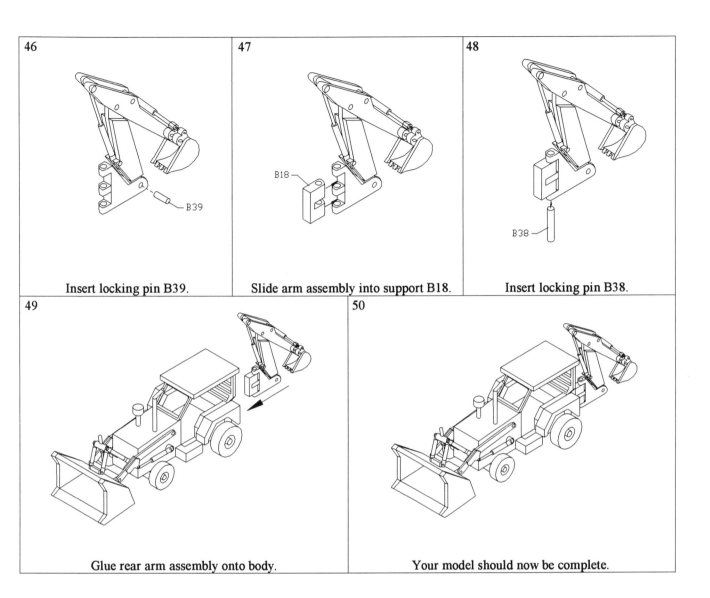

46	47	48
Insert locking pin B39.	Slide arm assembly into support B18.	Insert locking pin B38.

49	50
Glue rear arm assembly onto body.	Your model should now be complete.

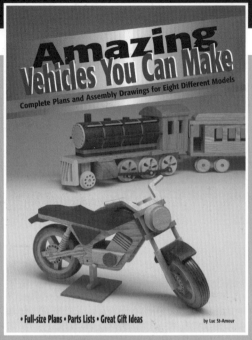
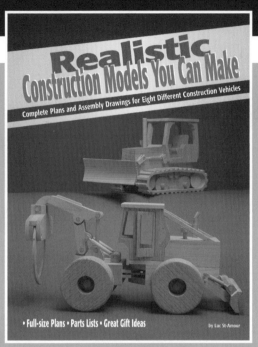
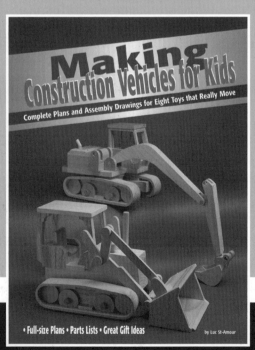
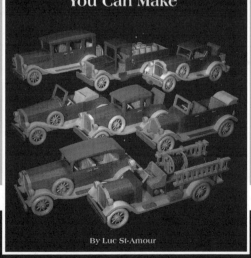